Praise for *Walking with Jesus*

"Magnificent. A beautiful invitation by a truly holy man to meet the one at the center of his life: Jesus Christ."
—James Martin, SJ, author of *Jesus: A Pilgrimage*

"Pope Francis knows that the encounter with Jesus Christ puts our lives on a new path. Our life of faith is a journey that we are making with Jesus—walking with him, sharing his life, traveling in the company of brothers and sisters who have accepted his invitation: 'Follow me.' In this inspiring book, our Holy Father offers us bread for the journey—to deepen our friendship with Jesus and our fellowship in continuing his mission of mercy in our world."
—Most Reverend José H. Gomez, Archbishop of Los Angeles

"A wonderfully inspiring and stirring resource capturing the depth of Pope Francis's magnificent vision and mission. His powerful message speaks of the richness of Catholic story and tradition. Walking with Jesus: A Way Forward for the Church *is an exceptional source of wisdom and guidance for all involved in the ministry of religious education."*
—Edith Prendergast, RSC, Director of Religious Education, Archdiocese of Los Angeles

Praise for *The Church of Mercy* by Pope Francis

"This collection offers fascinating insight into the mind and heart of someone who has rapidly become one of the world's most beloved public figures."
—Publishers Weekly

"Refreshingly humane, focusing on people rather than institutions. Admirers of Francis and students of Church history alike will find this a useful introduction to the pontiff's thought."
—Kirkus Reviews

"A magnificent book, bursting with profound spiritual insights, from a man who has quickly become one of the greatest spiritual teachers of our time."
—James Martin, SJ, author of *Jesus: A Pilgrimage*

"A refreshing book, a true treasure chest of wisdom, which will both comfort and unsettle any attentive reader."
—Englewood Review of Books

WALKING
with JESUS

A Way Forward for the Church

BY POPE FRANCIS

Foreword by
ARCHBISHOP BLASE J. CUPICH

LOYOLA PRESS.
A JESUIT MINISTRY
Chicago

LOYOLA PRESS.
A JESUIT MINISTRY

3441 N. Ashland Avenue
Chicago, Illinois 60657
(800) 621-1008
www.loyolapress.com

First published in English in 2015 by
Darton, Longman and Todd Ltd
1 Spencer Court
140–142 Wandsworth High Street
London SW18 4JJ

Published in Italian in 2014 by Edizione San Paolo
Piazza Soncino 5, 20092 Cinisello Balsamo (Mi), Italy

These documents in their original form, per Vatican Web site, contain ellipses. Any bracketed ellipses [. . .] indicate omissions chosen by the editor of this curation.

Cover art credit: Franco Origlia/GettyImages

Hardcover
ISBN-13: 978-0-8294-4248-9
ISBN-10: 0-8294-4248-0

Paperback
ISBN-13: 978-0-8294-4254-0
ISBN-10: 0-8294-4254-5
Library of Congress Control Number: 2015930346

Printed in the United States of America.
15 16 17 18 19 20 Bang 10 9 8 7 6 5 4 3 2 1

CONTENTS

Foreword

This is an important and needed book. It collects the words and teachings of Pope Francis under the intriguing theme of "walking with Jesus." The Gospels and the Acts of the Apostles describe the earliest disciples as those who walked with Jesus and referred to their life of faith as "the way." In these essays Pope Francis urges Christians in our time to take up the journey again and to renew their faith. But, more importantly, he shows us the way, as each of us struggles with the question: "How exactly do I walk with Jesus today?" The pope does so by drawing from the rich spiritual legacy of St. Ignatius of Loyola as well as his pastoral encounters across a long lifetime as a priest, bishop, and now pope.

St. Ignatius saw that the renewal and transformation of individuals and the Church could happen only by putting Christ in the center of our lives and by staying in his company. Under St. Ignatius's leadership, the earliest members of what would become the Society of Jesus also called themselves the "company of Jesus" and the "friends of Jesus." They were to be those who walked with Jesus by prayerfully moving through the mysteries of his life in the course of the Spiritual Exercises. They also walked with Jesus as his disciples and apostles who carried on the mission of Jesus in the Church and in the world.

The Ignatian vision of renewal began with those in the Society of Jesus, but it was destined to be a life-giving spiritual force for the entire Church. And Pope Francis clearly shares this spiritual heritage with the Church at large. All of us are summoned to walk with Jesus and to be his companions—the ones who share his life, his mission, and his destiny. At the same time, while we aspire to be companions of Jesus, we know that already he is our companion on the journey. He walks with us as a steady presence of hope and love when we make our pilgrim way, especially when we encounter difficulties and challenges.

As Pope Francis describes walking with Jesus, he also describes the surprisingly powerful impact of walking with him in our life together. Not only are we companions who walk with Jesus and not only is he our companion who walks with us, but in his company we also become companions to one another. This reality is so important in our cultural moment, which often is marked by a hypercompetitive spirit and is fixated on an unhealthy individualism, to the point that we are left feeling isolated as individuals and divided as a community. To walk with Jesus in the company of others describes the very essence of the Church. And reclaiming this reality will generate a true renewal of our life together.

Americans are practical people. When we think about renewal and transformation for a business, for a public institution, or even for the Church, we naturally gravitate to reorganizing structures. In our practicality and our can-do attitude, we often strain to figure things out and struggle to make things work. Pope Francis offers us an entirely different path for renewal, especially in the Church. For him, renewal is not about tinkering with structures or doing a new thing. Rather, it means reclaiming the centrality of Jesus Christ. And that, in turn, depends entirely on a new spirit and a new heart. The renewal that Pope Francis shows us is the conversion of heart that happens by walking with Jesus, by being in close contact with him. This is why he constantly insists that we read a passage of the Gospels day-by-day and reflect and pray on it, whether we are on public transport or at home. That is walking with Jesus.

When we make that kind of day-by-day commitment to walk with Jesus, we begin to live in a world of grace, depending on more than our human efforts. When Jesus walks with us and is our guide, Pope Francis tells us, we will keep discovering the deepest truth that makes us free and gives us life. The grace is already given to us to be uncovered, discovered, and embraced.

The vision of Pope Francis contained in these pages is not new. It is the perennial message of the Gospel. And although it is not new, he freshly proposes a way to be with Jesus in our time, to learn from him, and to draw life from him. And that is why I am convinced that many will be inspired and renewed by the blessed words of the Holy Father in this very important and needed book.

Blase J. Cupich
Archbishop of Chicago

Preface

All Is Walking

From the start of his pontificate, Pope Francis has most frequently used the image of walking. Just as for the writer Bernanos "All is grace," so for the pope "All is walking," meaning that every single action of a Christian is to be a step closer and closer to God and to one's neighbor. In Francis's vision, walking involves an image of the Church that goes outside itself, past its inner and outer walls, and reaches out to the people of the Lord and to the world. It is an image of an evangelizing Church, always on a mission, aware of the responsibility and joy of this walk; an image of a Church that is not afraid of the road or of what can be found among the people, especially on the outskirts of human existence, where cries of the poor, the marginalized, and the oppressed can be heard.

This walking Church is following the example of Jesus, who during his life walked all over Palestine, together with his disciples. Let us go back to those first times, to the surprise and the fear of those twelve men Jesus asked to give up everything and follow him. Let us in our turn reply, "Yes, we have met you; we want to stay and walk with you." They did not know where they would go and what they would find on the way, but they believed in him, they trusted him, and they threw themselves into what became not only the most shocking experience of their lives but also the greatest adventure in history. By walking, Jesus taught them what they needed to leave behind in order to be purified; he taught them to cleanse their hearts and understand what counts in the kingdom of God. Little by little, amid surprise and fear, falls and denials, they understood that their victory was to walk, to the end, the way of the cross, where Jesus had taken them, predicting his passion, death, and resurrection.

We never linger enough on the faith of the apostles and of the first disciples who, strengthened by Jesus' experience and their communion with him, started the long and never-ending walk of the mission, the Church's permanent goal. And we, who are linked historically and spiritually to the original Christian community, are again invited by Pope Francis to take up that walk: to resume it if we have stopped because we were tired or not entirely convinced of the goodness of the journey, or to start it from the beginning if we were not aware that faith means walking, being on the move.

Walking is, then, the process that sparks the search for the truth of the Gospel. This truth, once owned, obliges you to share it, bearing joyful witness to the newness of life it brings. Pope Francis's preaching is focused on explaining the final destination and the steps needed to get there, both on a personal level, for one's self-improvement and sanctification, and on a community level, for the building up of the Church upon its foundations of love, peace, and unity. As the Bible has it, "walk in him, rooted in him and built upon him" (Col. 2:6–7), according to "the law of the Spirit who gives life and freedom" (Rom. 8:2). If our desire is to walk "in newness of life" (Rom. 6:4), "in the light" (1 John 1:7), and "in love" (Eph. 5:2), then we need to know what must be removed and what must be the focus of the Christian life.

Vanity and hypocrisy, routine constraints, ingrained formalism, careerism, worldliness, triumphalism, idle chatter and complaints—all these must be got rid of because they affect the faith and the authenticity of our witness. These are underlying or clearly visible attitudes that Pope Francis has constantly and firmly criticized and that are the *leitmotiv* of his preaching. They belong with all the other behaviors he denounces, both in the Church and in society at large: abuse of power or money, corruption, consumerism, exploitation, wastefulness, excess, indifference, and offenses against human dignity of all kinds.

Jesus—his person and his message—needs to be central. The individual and interpersonal walk of the Christian is to learn that only this is necessary, and that it does not matter if we fall sometimes, if we then allow Jesus to help us up. His mercy, forgiveness, and faithful love—guidelines of Francis's pastoral vision—are the unfailing, loving touch of God, who gives solace, confidence, and hope, together with the courage to persevere and to keep walking.

We are never alone on this road. God is always ahead of us on the way, but not to impose rules that look like prohibitions that are an end in themselves, as we often view the commandments and the laws of the Church. Like Benedict XVI, Francis changes the perspective and shows how the limits imposed are not chains to imprison but, on the contrary, remedies that enable us to enter the sphere of the good and virtuous life according to God. The sacraments of the Christian initiation, the Eucharist, and all the other sacraments are the first indispensable means to establish in your life what St. Augustine called "the order of love." He referred to the conditions we need to lead a good life on earth and, at the same time, to look always toward the next world for which we are destined.

Besides, the gifts of the Holy Spirit come to our help, and this is another crucial topic of Francis's teaching. This matter, together with the sacraments, is amply covered in the following pages. The examples set by Mary, Joseph, and all the other saints comfort us during the difficulties of the walk. Getting to know them and appealing to them does not mean becoming like them, but it is helpful to thumb through the grammar of the Christian life, to go deeper into Jesus' mystery and to learn how to live. Most of all, a wave of prayer must rise from the heart because we cannot live as Christians without praying. Prayer is the bridge that connects us to God, whom we can ask for "bread," forgiveness, and help in the hour of temptation, with the certainty of those who see, in God, the Father of each and every one.

Pope Francis sets us on this way of spirituality and discernment in the Church, giving us courage and hope. His priestly fatherhood and pastoral simplicity, his straightforward, friendly, and lively speaking style light up people's hearts and naturally build strong spiritual bonds. This happens despite the strong messages and stern denouncements he makes constantly to remind us that the Christian life is a struggle with ourselves and with evil. In his homilies and speeches there is always a message of confidence and joy that makes the fight less hard and turns the Way—in its spiritual and pastoral sense—into the place of meeting for those who live in the communion and fellowship of faith.

Giuliano Vigini

PART ONE

The Gospel of the Walk

1

A Journey Unfolding in Time

From the encyclical Lumen Fidei *("The Light of Faith"),*
June 29, 2013

In faith, Christ is not simply the one in whom we believe, the supreme manifestation of God's love; he is also the one with whom we are united precisely *in order* to believe. Faith does not merely gaze at Jesus, but sees things as Jesus himself sees them, with his own eyes: it is a participation in his way of seeing. In many areas of our lives we trust others who know more than we do. We trust the architect who builds our home, the pharmacist who gives us medicine for healing, the lawyer who defends us in court. We also need someone trustworthy and knowledgeable where God is concerned. Jesus, the Son of God, is the one who makes God known to us (cf. John 1:18). Christ's life, his way of knowing the Father and living in complete and constant relationship with him, opens up new and inviting vistas for human experience. St. John brings out the importance of a personal relationship with Jesus for our faith by using various forms of the verb "to believe." In addition to "believing that" what Jesus tells us is true (cf. John 14:10; 20:31), John also speaks of "believing" Jesus and "believing in" Jesus. We "believe" Jesus when we accept his word, his testimony, because he is truthful (cf. John 6:30). We "believe in" Jesus when we personally welcome him into our lives and journey toward him, clinging to him in love and following in his footsteps along the way (cf. John 2:11; 6:47; 12:44).

To enable us to know, accept, and follow him, the Son of God took on our flesh. In this way he also saw the Father humanly, within the setting of a journey unfolding in time. Christian faith is faith in the incarnation of the Word and his bodily resurrection; it is faith in a God who is so close to us that he entered our human history.

> *Christ's life, his way of knowing the Father and living in complete and constant relationship with him, opens up new and inviting vistas for human experience.*

Far from divorcing us from reality, our faith in the Son of God made man in Jesus of Nazareth enables us to grasp reality's deepest meaning and to see how much God loves this world and is constantly guiding it toward himself. This leads us, as Christians, to live in this world with ever greater commitment and intensity.

On the basis of this sharing in Jesus' way of seeing things, St. Paul has left us a description of the life of faith. In accepting the gift of faith, believers become a new creation; they receive a new being; as God's children, they are now "sons in the Son." The phrase "*Abba*, Father," so characteristic of Jesus' own experience, now becomes the core of the Christian experience (cf. Rom. 8:15). The life of faith, as a filial existence, is the acknowledgment of a primordial and radical gift that upholds our lives.

We see this clearly in St. Paul's question to the Corinthians: "What do you have that you did not receive?" (1 Cor. 4:7). This was at the very heart of Paul's debate with the Pharisees: the issue of whether salvation is attained by faith or by the works of the law. Paul rejects the attitude of those who would consider themselves justified before God on the basis of their own works. Such people, even when they obey the commandments and do good works, are centered on themselves; they fail to realize that goodness comes from God. Those who live this way, who want to be the source of their own righteousness, find that the latter is soon depleted and that they are unable even to keep the law. They become closed in on themselves and isolated from the Lord and from others; their lives become futile and their works barren, like a tree far from water.

St. Augustine tells us in his usual concise and striking way: "*Ab eo qui fecit te, noli deficere nec ad te*": "Do not turn away from the one who made you, even to turn toward yourself." Once I think that by turning away from God I will find myself, my life begins to fall apart (cf. Luke 15:11–24). The beginning of salvation is openness to something prior to ourselves, to a primordial gift that affirms life and sustains it in being. Only by being open to and acknowledging this gift can we be transformed, experience salvation, and bear good fruit.

Salvation by faith means recognizing the primacy of God's gift. As St. Paul puts it, "By grace you have been saved through faith, and this is not your own doing; it is the gift of God" (Eph. 2:8). Faith's new way of seeing things is centered on Christ. Faith in Christ brings salvation because in him our lives become radically open to a love that precedes us, a love that transforms us from within, acting in us and through us.

This is seen clearly in St. Paul's exegesis of a text from Deuteronomy, an exegesis consonant with the heart of the Old Testament message. Moses tells the people that God's command is neither too high nor too far away. There is no need to say, "Who will go up for us to heaven and bring it to us?" or "Who will go over the sea for us, and bring it to us?" (Deut. 30:11–14). Paul interprets this nearness of God's word in terms of Christ's presence in the Christian. "Do not say in your heart, 'Who will ascend into heaven?' (that is, to bring Christ down), or 'Who will descend into the abyss?' (that is, to bring Christ up from the dead)" (Rom. 10:6–7). Christ came down to earth and rose from the dead; by his incarnation and resurrection, the Son of God embraced the whole of human life and history and now dwells in our hearts through the Holy Spirit. Faith knows that God has drawn close to us, that Christ has been given to us as a great gift that inwardly transforms us, dwells within us, and thus bestows on us the light that illumines the origin and the end of life.

We come to see the difference, then, that faith makes for us. Those who believe are transformed by the love to which they have opened their hearts in faith. By their openness to this offer of primordial love, their lives are enlarged and expanded. "It is no longer I who live, but Christ who lives in me" (Gal. 2:20). "May Christ dwell in your hearts through faith" (Eph. 3:17). The self-awareness of the believer now expands because of the presence of another; it now lives in this other and thus, in love, life takes on a whole new breadth. Here we see the Holy Spirit at work. The Christian can see with the eyes of Jesus and share in his mind, his filial disposition, because he or she shares in his love, which is the Spirit. In the love of Jesus, we receive his vision in a certain way. Without being conformed to him in love, without the presence of the Spirit, it is impossible to confess him as Lord (cf. 1 Cor. 12:3).

In this way, the life of the believer becomes an ecclesial existence, a life lived in the Church. When St. Paul tells the Christians of Rome that all who believe in Christ make up one body, he urges them not to boast of this; rather, each must think of himself "according to the measure of faith that God has assigned" (Rom. 12:3). Those who believe come to see themselves in the light of the faith they profess: Christ is the mirror in which they find their own image fully realized. And just as Christ gathers to himself all those who believe and makes them his body, so the Christian comes to see himself or herself as a member of this body, in an essential relationship with all other believers.

The image of a body does not imply that the believer is simply one part of an anonymous whole, a mere cog in a great machine; rather, it brings out the vital union of Christ with believers and of believers among themselves (cf. Rom. 12:4–5). Christians are "one" (cf. Gal. 3:28) but in a way that does not make them lose their individuality; in service to others, they come into their own in the highest degree. This explains why, apart from this body, outside this unity of the Church in Christ, outside this Church that, in the words of Romano Guardini, "is the bearer within history of the plenary gaze of Christ on the world," faith loses its "measure"; it no longer finds its equilibrium, the space needed to sustain itself.

Faith is necessarily ecclesial; it is professed from within the Body of Christ as a concrete communion of believers. It is against this ecclesial backdrop that faith opens the individual Christian toward all others. Christ's word, once heard, by virtue of its inner power at work in the heart of the Christian, becomes a response, a spoken word, a profession of faith. As St. Paul puts it, "one believes with the heart . . . and confesses with the lips" (Rom. 10:10).

Faith is not a private matter, a completely individualistic notion or a personal opinion: it comes from hearing, and it is meant to find expression in words and to be proclaimed. For "how are they to believe in him of whom they have never heard? And how are they to hear without a preacher?" (Rom. 10:14). Faith becomes operative in the Christian on the basis of the gift received, the love that attracts our hearts to Christ (cf. Gal. 5:6) and enables us to become part of the Church's great pilgrimage through history until the end of the world. For those who have been transformed in this way, a new way of seeing opens up, and faith becomes light for their eyes.

3

Three Movements of the Christian Life

Homily for the Mass with the cardinals, March 14, 2013

e three readings [for today's Mass], I see a common element: that of
ent. In the first reading, it is the movement of a journey; in the second
, the movement of building the Church; in the third, in the Gospel,
vement involved in professing the faith.
neying. "O house of Jacob, come, let us walk in the light of the Lord"
5). This is the first thing God said to Abraham: Walk in my pres-
d live blamelessly. Journeying: our life is a journey, and when we stop
, things go wrong. Always [we are] journeying, in the presence of the
n the light of the Lord, seeking to live with the blamelessness that God
f Abraham in his promise.
ding. We are building the Church. We speak of stones. Stones are
ut living stones are stones anointed by the Holy Spirit. We are build-
Church, the Bride of Christ, on the cornerstone that is the Lord him-
his is another kind of movement in our lives: building.
fessing. We can walk as much as we want, and we can build many
, but if we do not profess Jesus Christ, things go wrong. We may
e a charitable non-governmental organization but not the Church, the
of the Lord. When we are not walking, we stop moving. When we are
ilding on the stones, what happens? The same thing that happens to
en on the beach when they build sand castles: everything is swept away,

2

The Eternal Newness of the Gospel

From the apostolic exhortation Evangelii Gaudium
("The Joy of the Gospel"), November 24, 2013

A renewal of preaching can offer believers, as well as the lukewarm and the non-practicing, new joy in the faith and fruitfulness in the work of evangelization. The heart of its message will always be the same: God revealed his immense love in the crucified and risen Christ.

God constantly renews his faithful ones, whatever their age: "They shall mount up with wings like eagles, they shall run and not be weary, they shall walk and not be faint" (Isa. 40:31). Christ is the "eternal Gospel" (Rev. 14:6); he "is the same yesterday and today and forever" (Heb. 13:8), yet his riches and beauty are inexhaustible. He is forever young and a constant source of newness.

The Church never fails to be amazed at "the depth of the riches and wisdom and knowledge of God" (Rom. 11:33). St. John of the Cross says that "the thicket of God's wisdom and knowledge is so deep and so broad that the soul, however much it has come to know of it, can always penetrate deeper within it." Or as St. Irenaeus writes: "By his coming, Christ brought with him all newness." With this newness he is always able to renew our lives and our communities, and even if the Christian message has known periods of darkness and ecclesial weakness, it will never grow old.

Jesus can also break through the dull categories with which we would enclose him, and he constantly amazes us by his divine creativity. Whenever we make the effort to return to the source and to recover the original freshness of the Gospel, new avenues arise, new paths of creativity open up, with different forms of expression, more eloquent signs, and words with new Every form of authentic evangelization is always

In thes
movem
reading
the mo

Jou
(Isa. 2:
ence a
movin
Lord,
asked

Bu
solid,
ing th
self. T

Pro
things
becom
Bride
not b
child

there is no solidity. When we do not profess Jesus Christ, the saying of Léon Bloy comes to mind: "Anyone who does not pray to the Lord prays to the devil." When we do not profess Jesus Christ, we profess the worldliness of the devil, a demonic worldliness.

Journeying, building, professing. But things are not so straightforward, because in journeying, building, and professing there can sometimes be jolts, movements that are not properly part of the journey, movements that pull us back.

This Gospel continues with a situation of a particular kind. The same Peter who professed Jesus Christ now says to him: You are the Christ, the Son of the living God. I will follow you, but let us not speak of the cross. That has nothing to do with it. I will follow you on other terms, but without the cross. When we journey without the cross, when we build without the cross, when we profess Christ without the cross, we are not disciples of the Lord, we are worldly. We may be bishops, priests, cardinals, popes, but not disciples of the Lord.

When we journey without the cross, when we build without the cross, when we profess Christ without the cross, we are not disciples of the Lord, we are worldly.

My wish is that all of us [. . .] will have the courage, yes, the courage, to walk in the presence of the Lord, with the Lord's cross; to build the Church on the Lord's blood, which was poured out on the cross; and to profess the one glory: Christ crucified. And in this way, the Church will go forward.

My prayer for all of us is that the Holy Spirit, through the intercession of the Blessed Virgin Mary, our Mother, will grant us this grace: to walk, to build, and to profess Jesus Christ crucified.

4

Walking with Jesus

Homily at the Public Consistory for the Creation of New Cardinals,
February 22, 2014

"Jesus *was walking ahead* of them." (Mark 10:32).

At this moment, too, Jesus is walking ahead of us. He is always before us. He goes ahead of us and leads the way. . . . This is the source of our confidence and our joy: to be his disciples, to remain with him, to walk behind him, to follow him. . . .

[T]o walk is [. . .] an action, an action of Jesus that is ongoing: "Jesus *was walking* . . ." This is something striking about the Gospels: Jesus is often walking, and he teaches his disciples along the way. This is important. Jesus did not come to teach a philosophy, an ideology . . . but rather "a way," a journey to be undertaken with him, and we learn the way as we go, by walking. Yes, [. . .] this is our joy: to walk with Jesus.

And this is not easy, or comfortable, because the way Jesus chooses is the way of the cross. As they journey together, he speaks to his disciples about what will happen in Jerusalem: he foretells his passion, death, and resurrection. And they are "shocked" and "full of fear." They were shocked, certainly, because for them going up to Jerusalem meant sharing in the triumph of the Messiah, in his victory—we see this in the request made by James and John [to sit on either side of him in

> *Jesus did not come to teach a philosophy, an ideology but rather "a way," a journey to be undertaken with him, and we learn the way as we go, by walking.*

his kingdom]. But they were also full of fear for what was about to happen to Jesus, and for what they themselves might have to endure.

Unlike the disciples in those days, we know that Jesus has won, and that we need not fear the cross; indeed, the cross is our hope. And yet, we are all too human, sinners, tempted to think as people do, not as God does.

And once we follow the thinking of the world, what happens? The Gospel tells us: "When the ten heard it, they began *to be indignant* at James and John" (Mark 10:41). They were indignant. Whenever a worldly mentality predominates, the result is rivalry, jealousy, factions. . . . And so the word Jesus speaks to us today is most salutary. It purifies us inwardly, it enlightens our consciences and helps us to unite ourselves fully with Jesus, and to do so together. [. . .]

"And Jesus *called them to himself*" (Mark 10:42). Here is the other action of Jesus. Along the way, he is aware that he needs to speak to the Twelve; he stops and calls them to himself. [. . .] Let us allow Jesus to call us to himself! Let us be "con-voked" by him. And let us listen to him, with the joy that comes from receiving his word together, from letting ourselves be taught by that word and by the Holy Spirit, and to become ever more of one heart and soul, gathered around him.

And as we are thus "con-voked," "called to himself" by our one Teacher, I will tell you what the Church needs: she needs you, your cooperation, and even more your communion, with me and among yourselves. The Church needs your courage, to proclaim the Gospel at all times, both in season and out of season, and to bear witness to the truth. The Church needs your prayer for the progress of Christ's flock, that prayer—let us not forget this!—which, along with the proclamation of the Word, is the primary task of the bishop.

The Church needs your compassion, especially at this time of pain and suffering for so many countries throughout the world. Let us together express our spiritual closeness to the ecclesial communities and to all Christians suffering from discrimination and persecution. We must fight every form of discrimination! The Church needs our prayer for them, that they may be firm in faith and capable of responding to evil with good. And this prayer of ours extends to every man and woman suffering injustice on account of their religious convictions.

The Church needs us also to be peacemakers, building peace by our words, our hopes, and our prayers. Building peace! Being peacemakers! Let us therefore invoke peace and reconciliation for those peoples presently experiencing violence, exclusion, and war.

Let us walk together behind the Lord, and let us always be called together by him, in the midst of his faithful people, the holy People of God, holy Mother the Church.

5

The Joy of Encounter

From the apostolic exhortation Evangelii Gaudium
("The Joy of the Gospel"), November 24, 2013

The joy of the Gospel fills the hearts and lives of all who encounter Jesus. Those who accept his offer of salvation are set free from sin, sorrow, inner emptiness, and loneliness. With Christ joy is constantly born anew. [. . .]

The great danger in today's world, pervaded as it is by consumerism, is the desolation and anguish born of a complacent yet covetous heart, the feverish pursuit of frivolous pleasures, and a blunted conscience. Whenever our interior life becomes caught up in its own interests and concerns, there is no longer room for others, no place for the poor. God's voice is no longer heard, the quiet joy of his love is no longer felt, and the desire to do good fades. This is a very real danger for believers, too. Many fall prey to it and end up resentful, angry, and listless. That is no way to live a dignified and fulfilled life; it is not God's will for us, nor is it the life in the Spirit, which has its source in the heart of the risen Christ.

I invite all Christians, everywhere, at this very moment, to a renewed personal encounter with Jesus Christ, or at least an openness to letting him encounter them. I ask all of you to do this unfailingly each day. No one should think that this invitation is not meant for him or her because "no one is excluded from the joy brought by the Lord."

The Lord does not disappoint those who take this risk; whenever we take a step toward Jesus, we come to realize that he is already there, waiting for us with open arms. Now is the time to say to Jesus: "Lord, I have let myself be deceived; in a thousand ways I have shunned your love. Yet here I am once more, to renew my covenant with you. I need you. Save me once again, Lord, take me once more into your redeeming embrace." How good it feels to come back to him whenever we are lost!

Let me say this once more: God never tires of forgiving us; we are the ones who tire of seeking his mercy. Christ, who told us to forgive one another "seventy times seven" (Matt. 18:22), has given us his example: he has forgiven us seventy times seven. Time and time again he bears us on his shoulders. No one can strip us of the dignity bestowed upon us by this boundless and unfailing love. With a tenderness that never disappoints but is always capable of restoring our joy, he makes it possible for us to lift up our heads and start anew. Let us not flee from the resurrection of Jesus; let us never give up, come what will. May nothing inspire [us] more than his life, which impels us onward!

> *Time and time again he bears us on his shoulders. No one can strip us of the dignity bestowed upon us by this boundless and unfailing love.*

PART TWO

The Walk of Faith

6

The Sacraments: Life and Sustenance for the Way

From the encyclical Lumen Fidei *("The Light of Faith"),*
June 29, 2013

The Church, like every family, passes on to her children the whole store of her memories. But how does this come about in a way that nothing is lost, but rather everything in the patrimony of faith comes to be more deeply understood? It is through the apostolic tradition preserved in the Church with the assistance of the Holy Spirit that we enjoy a living contact with the foundational memory. What was handed down by the apostles—as the Second Vatican Council states—"comprises everything that serves to make the people of God live their lives in holiness and increase their faith. In this way the Church, in her doctrine, life, and worship, perpetuates and transmits to every generation all that she herself is, all that she believes."

Faith, in fact, needs a setting in which it can be witnessed to and communicated, a means suitable and proportionate to what is communicated. For transmitting a purely doctrinal content, an idea might suffice, or perhaps a book, or the repetition of a spoken message. But what is communicated in the Church, what is handed down in her living tradition, is the new light born of an encounter with the true God, a light that touches us at the core of our being and engages our minds, wills, and emotions, opening us to relationships lived in communion.

There is a special means for passing down this fullness, a means capable of engaging the entire person, body and spirit, interior life and relationships with others. [This transmission comes to us by way of] the sacraments, celebrated in the Church's liturgy. The sacraments communicate an incarnate memory, linked to the times and places of our lives, linked to all our senses; in them the whole person is engaged as a member of a living subject and part of a network of communitarian relationships. While the sacraments are indeed sacraments of faith, it can also be said that faith itself possesses a sacramental structure. The awakening of faith is linked to the dawning of a new sacramental sense in our lives as human beings and as Christians, in which visible and material realities are seen to point beyond themselves to the mystery of the eternal.

The transmission of faith occurs first and foremost in baptism. Some might think that baptism is merely a way of symbolizing the confession of faith, a pedagogical tool for those who require images and signs, while in itself it is ultimately unnecessary. An observation of St. Paul about baptism reminds us that this is not the case. Paul states that "we were buried with him by baptism into death, so that, just as Christ was raised from the dead by the glory of the Father, we too might [walk] in newness of life" (Rom. 6:4).

> *The sacraments communicate an incarnate memory, linked to the times and places of our lives, linked to all our senses.*

In baptism we become a new creation and God's adopted children. The apostle goes on to say that Christians have been entrusted to a "standard of teaching" (*týpos didachés*), which they now obey from the heart (cf. Rom. 6:17). In baptism we receive both a teaching to be professed and a specific way of life that demands the engagement of the whole person and sets us on the path to goodness. Those who are baptized are set in a new context, entrusted to a new environment, a new and shared way of acting, in the Church. Baptism makes us see, then, that faith is not the achievement of isolated individuals; it is not an act someone can perform on his or her own, but rather something that must be received by entering into the ecclesial communion that transmits God's gift. No one baptizes himself, just as no one comes into the world by himself. Baptism is something we receive.

What are the elements of baptism that introduce us into this new "standard of teaching"? First, the name of the Trinity—the Father, the Son, and the Holy Spirit—is invoked upon the catechumen. Thus, from the outset, a synthesis of the journey of faith is provided. The God who called Abraham and wished to be called his God, the God who revealed his name to Moses, the God who, in giving us his Son, revealed fully the mystery of his Name, now bestows upon the baptized a new filial identity.

This is seen clearly in the act of baptism itself: immersion in water. Water is at once a symbol of death, inviting us to pass through self-conversion to a new and greater identity, and a symbol of life, of a womb in which we are reborn by following Christ in his new life. In this way, through immersion in water, baptism speaks to us of the incarnational structure of faith. Christ's work penetrates the depths of our being and transforms us radically, making us adopted children of God and sharers in the divine nature. Baptism thus modifies all our relationships, our place in this world and in the universe, and opens them to God's own life of communion. This change that takes place in baptism helps us appreciate the singular importance of the catechumenate—whereby growing numbers of adults, even in societies with ancient Christian roots, now approach the sacrament of baptism—for the new evangelization. It is the road of preparation for baptism, for the transformation of our whole life in Christ.

To appreciate this link between baptism and faith, we can recall a text of the prophet Isaiah, which was associated with baptism in early Christian literature: "Their refuge will be the fortresses of rocks . . . their water assured" (Isa. 33:16). The baptized, rescued from the waters of death, were now set on a "fortress of rock" because they had found a firm and reliable foundation. The waters of death were thus transformed into waters of life. The Greek text, in speaking of that water that is "assured," uses the word *pistós*: "faithful." The waters of baptism are indeed faithful and trustworthy, for they flow with the power of Christ's love, the source of our assurance in the journey of life.

The structure of baptism—its form as a rebirth in which we receive a new name and a new life—helps us appreciate the meaning and importance of infant baptism. Children are not capable of accepting the faith by a free act; nor are they yet able to profess that faith on their own. Therefore the faith is professed by their parents and godparents in their name. Since faith is a reality lived within the community of the Church, part of a common "we," children can be supported by others, their parents and godparents, and welcomed into their faith, which is the faith of the Church. This is symbolized by the candle that the child's father lights from the paschal candle.

The structure of baptism, then, demonstrates the critical importance of cooperation between Church and family in passing on the faith. Parents are called, as St. Augustine once said, not only to bring children into the world but also to bring them to God, so that through baptism they can be reborn as children of God and receive the gift of faith. Thus, along with life, children are given a fundamental orientation and assured of a good future; this orientation will be strengthened further in the sacrament of confirmation with the seal of the Holy Spirit.

The sacramental character of faith finds its highest expression in the Eucharist. The Eucharist is a precious nourishment for faith: an encounter with Christ truly present in the supreme act of his love, the life-giving gift of himself.

In the Eucharist we find the intersection of faith's two dimensions. On the one hand, there is the dimension of history: the Eucharist is an act of remembrance, a making present of the mystery in which the past, as an event of death and resurrection, demonstrates its ability to open up a future, to foreshadow ultimate fulfillment. The liturgy reminds us of this by its repetition of the word *hodie*, the "today" of the mysteries of salvation. On the other hand, we also find the dimension that leads from the visible world to the invisible. In the Eucharist we learn to see the heights and depths of reality. The bread and wine are changed into the body and blood of Christ, who becomes present in his Passover to the Father. This movement draws us, body and soul, into the movement of all creation toward its fulfillment in God.

In the celebration of the sacraments, the Church hands down her memory especially through the profession of faith. The Creed involves not only giving one's assent to a body of abstract truths; rather, when it is recited, the whole of life is drawn into a journey towards full communion with the living God. We can say that in the Creed believers are invited to enter into the mystery they profess and to be transformed by it.

To understand what this means, let us look first at the contents of the Creed. It has a Trinitarian structure: the Father and the Son are united in the Spirit of love. The believer thus states that the core of all being, the inmost secret of all reality, is the divine communion. The Creed also contains a Christological confession: it takes us through all the mysteries of Christ's life up to his death, resurrection, and ascension into heaven before his final return in glory. It tells us that this God of communion, reciprocal love between the Father and the Son in the Spirit, is capable of embracing all of human history and drawing it into the dynamic unity of the Godhead, which has its source and fulfillment in the Father.

The believer who professes his or her faith is taken up, as it were, into the truth being professed. He or she cannot truthfully recite the words of the Creed without being changed, without becoming part of that history of love that embraces us and expands our being, making it part of a great fellowship, the ultimate subject that recites the Creed—namely, the Church. All the truths in which we believe point to the mystery of the new life of faith as a journey of communion with the living God.

7

Baptism: The Beginning

General Audience, January 8, 2014

Baptism is the sacrament on which our very faith is founded and which grafts us as living members onto Christ and his Church. Together with the Eucharist and confirmation, it forms what is known as "Christian initiation," like one great sacramental event that configures us to the Lord and turns us into a living sign of his presence and of his love.

Yet a question may stir within us: is baptism really necessary to live as Christians and follow Jesus? After all, isn't it merely a ritual, a formal act of the Church in order to give a name to the little boy or girl? This question can arise. And on this point, what the apostle Paul writes is illuminating: "Do you not know that all of us who have been baptized into Christ Jesus were baptized into his death? We were buried therefore with him by baptism into death, so that as Christ was raised from the dead by the glory of the Father, we too might walk in newness of life" (Rom. 6:3–4). Therefore, it is not a formality! It is an act that touches the depths of our existence. A baptized child and an unbaptized child are not the same. A person who is baptized and a person who is not baptized are not the same. We, by baptism, are immersed in that inexhaustible source of life, which is the death of Jesus, the greatest act of love in all of history. And thanks to this love we can live a new life, no longer at the mercy of evil, of sin, and of death, but in communion with God and with our brothers and sisters.

Many of us have no memory of the celebration of this sacrament, and it is obvious why, if we were baptized soon after birth. I have asked this question two or three times already [. . .]: who among you knows the date of your baptism? It is important to know the day on which you were immersed in that current of Jesus' salvation. And I will allow myself to give you some advice . . . but, more than advice, a task. Today, at home, ask about the date of your baptism; that way you will keep in mind that most beautiful day. To know the date of our baptism is to know a blessed day.

The danger of not knowing [the date of our baptism] is that we can lose awareness of what the Lord has done in us, the memory of the gift we have received. Thus, we end up considering it merely as an event that took place in the past—and not by our own will but by that of our parents—and that it has no impact on the present. We must reawaken the memory of our baptism. We are called to live out our baptism every day as the present reality of our lives. If we manage to follow Jesus and to remain in the Church, despite our limitations and with our weaknesses and our sins, it is precisely in the sacrament whereby we have become new creatures and have been clothed in Christ.

It is by the power of baptism, in fact, that, freed of original sin, we are included, gathered into, Jesus' relation to God the Father; that we are bearers of a new hope, for baptism gives us this new hope: the hope of going on the path of salvation our whole life long. And this hope nothing and no one can extinguish, for it is a hope that does not disappoint. Remember, hope in the Lord never disappoints. Thanks to baptism, we are capable of forgiving and of loving even those who offend us and do evil to us. By our baptism, we recognize in the least and in the poor the face of the Lord who visits us and makes himself close. Baptism helps us recognize in the face of the needy, of the suffering, and also of our neighbor, the face of Jesus. All this is possible thanks to the power of baptism!

A last point, which is important. I ask you a question: can a person baptize him or herself? No one can be self-baptized! No one. We can ask for it, desire it, but we always need someone else to confer this sacrament in the name of the Lord. For baptism is a gift bestowed in a context of care and fraternal sharing. Throughout history, one baptizes another, another, and another . . . it is a chain, a chain of grace. I cannot baptize myself: I must ask another for baptism. It is an act of brotherhood, an act of filiation to the Church.

> *It is by the power of baptism that, freed of original sin, we are gathered into Jesus' relation to God the Father; that we are bearers of a new hope, of going on the path of salvation our whole life long.*

In the celebration of baptism we can see the most genuine features of the Church, who like a mother continues to give birth to new children in Christ, in the fecundity of the Holy Spirit. Let us, then, ask the Lord from our hearts that we may be able to experience ever more, in everyday life, this grace that we have received at baptism. That in encountering us, our brothers and sisters may encounter true children of God, true brothers and sisters of Jesus Christ, true members of the Church. And do not forget your homework today: find out the date of your baptism. As I know my birthday, I should know my baptism day, because it is a feast day.

8

Grace from Generation to Generation

General Audience, January 15, 2014

I would like to pause again on the topic of baptism today, in order to stress an important fruit of this sacrament: it makes us members of the Body of Christ and of the People of God. St. Thomas Aquinas states that whoever receives baptism is incorporated in Christ, almost as one of his own limbs, and becomes aggregated to the community of the faithful (cf. *Summa Theologiae*, III, q. 69, art. 5; q. 70, art. 1), that is, the People of God. In the school of the Second Vatican Council, we say today that baptism allows us *to enter the People of God*, to become members of *a people on a journey*, a people on pilgrimage through history.

In effect, as from generation to generation life is transmitted, so too from generation to generation, through rebirth at the baptismal font, grace is transmitted, and by this grace the Christian people journey through time, like a river that irrigates the land and spreads God's blessing throughout the world. From the moment that Jesus said what we heard in today's Gospel reading, the disciples went out to baptize, and from that time until today there is a chain in the transmission of the faith through baptism. And each one of us is a link in that chain: a step forward, always, like a river that irrigates. Such is the grace of God and such is our faith, which we must transmit to our sons and daughters, transmit to children, so that once adults, they can do the same for their children. This is what baptism is. Why? Because baptism lets us enter this People of God that transmits the faith. This is very important. A People of God that journeys and hands down the faith.

In virtue of baptism we become *missionary disciples*, called to bring the Gospel to the world (cf. apostolic exhortation *Evangelii Gaudium*, n. 120). "All the baptized, whatever their position in the Church or their level of instruction in the faith, are agents of evangelization. . . . The new evangelization calls for personal involvement" (*ibid.*) from everyone, the whole of the People of God, a new kind of personal involvement on the part of each of the baptized. The People of God are a *disciple people* because

> *From generation to generation, through rebirth at the baptismal font, grace is transmitted, and by this grace the Christian people journeys through time, like a river that irrigates the land and spreads God's blessing throughout the world.*

they receive the faith, and they are a *missionary people* because they transmit the faith. And this is what baptism works in us: it gives us grace and hands on the faith to us. All of us in the Church are disciples, and this we are forever, our whole life long; and we are all missionaries, each in the place the Lord has assigned to him or her. Everyone: the littlest one is also a missionary, and the one who seems to be the greatest is a disciple.

But one of you might say, "Bishops are not disciples; bishops know everything. The pope knows everything; he is not a disciple." No, the bishops and the pope must also be disciples, because if they are not disciples, they do no good. They cannot be missionaries, they cannot transmit the faith. We must all be disciples and missionaries.

There exists an indissoluble bond between the *mystical* and the *missionary* dimension of the Christian vocation; both are rooted in baptism. "Upon receiving faith and Baptism, we Christians accept the action of the Holy Spirit who leads to confessing Jesus as Son of God and calling God '*Abba*,' Father. . . . All of us who are baptized . . . are called to live and transmit communion with the Trinity, for evangelization is a calling to participate in the communion of the Trinity" (*Final Document of Aparecida*, n. 157).

No one is saved by himself or herself. We are the community of believers, we are the People of God, and in this community we share the beauty of the experience of a love that precedes us all, but that at the same time calls us to be "channels" of grace for one another, despite our limitations and our sins. The communitarian dimension is not just a "frame," an "outline," but an integral part of Christian life, of witness and of evangelization. The Christian faith is born and lives in the Church, and in baptism families and parishes celebrate the incorporation of a new member in Christ and in his Body which is the Church (cf. *ibid.*, n. 175b).

On the subject of the importance of baptism for the People of God, the history of the Christian community in Japan is exemplary. It suffered severe persecution at the start of the seventeenth century. There were many martyrs; members of the clergy were expelled and thousands of faithful killed. No priest was left in Japan—they were all expelled. Then the community retreated into hiding, keeping the faith and prayer in seclusion. And when a child was born, the father or mother baptized him or her, because the faithful can baptize in certain circumstances.

When, after roughly two and a half centuries, missionaries returned to Japan, thousands of Christians stepped out into the open, and the Church was able to flourish again. They survived by the grace of baptism! This is profound: the People of God transmit the faith, baptize her children, and go forward. And they maintained, even in secret, a strong communal spirit because their baptism had made of them one single body in Christ. They were isolated and hidden, but they were always members of the People of God, members of the Church. Let us learn a great deal from this history!

9

Confirmation: Crucial to Our Continuing

General Audience, January 29, 2014

We pause to reflect on confirmation, or "chrismation," which must be understood in continuity with baptism, to which it is inseparably linked. These two sacraments, together with the Eucharist, form a single saving event—called "Christian initiation"—in which we are incorporated into Jesus Christ, who died and rose, and become new creatures and members of the Church. This is why these three sacraments were originally celebrated on one occasion, at the end of the catechumenal journey, normally at the Easter Vigil. The path of formation and gradual integration into the Christian community, which could last even up to a few years, was thus sealed. One travelled step by step to reach baptism, then confirmation and the Eucharist.

We commonly speak of the sacrament of *chrismation*, a word that signifies "anointing." And, in effect, through the oil called "sacred chrism" we are conformed, in the power of the Spirit, to Jesus Christ, who is the only true "anointed One," the Messiah, the Holy One of God. The word *confirmation* then reminds us that this sacrament brings an increase and deepening of baptismal grace. It unites us more firmly to Christ, it renders our bond with the Church more perfect, and it gives us a special strength of the Holy Spirit to spread and defend the faith . . . to confess the name of Christ boldly, and never to be ashamed of his cross (cf. *Catechism of the Catholic Church*, n. 1303).

For this reason, it is important to take care that our children, our young people, receive this sacrament. We all take care that they are baptized, and this is good, but perhaps we do not take so much care to ensure that they are confirmed. Thus they remain at a midpoint in their journey and do not receive the Holy Spirit, who is so important in the Christian life because he gives us the strength to go on. Let us think a little, each one of us: do we truly care whether our children, our young people, receive confirmation? This is important! And if you have children or adolescents at home who have not yet received it and are at the age to do so, do everything possible to ensure that they complete their Christian initiation and receive the power of the Holy Spirit.

Naturally it is important to prepare well those being confirmed, leading them toward a personal commitment to faith in Christ and reawakening in them a sense of belonging to the Church. Confirmation, like every sacrament, is not the work of human beings but of God, who cares for our lives in such a manner as to mold us in the image of his Son, to make us capable of loving as he loves. He does this by infusing in us his Holy Spirit, whose action pervades the whole person and his or her entire life, as reflected in the seven gifts that tradition, in light of the sacred Scripture, has always highlighted. What are these gifts? Wisdom, understanding, counsel, fortitude, knowledge, piety, and fear of the Lord. And these gifts have been given to us precisely with the Holy Spirit in the sacrament of confirmation.

When we welcome the Holy Spirit into our hearts and allow him to act, Christ makes himself present in us and takes shape in our lives; through us, it will be Christ himself who prays, forgives, gives hope and consolation, serves our brothers and sisters, draws close to the needy and to the least, creates community, and sows peace. Think how important this is: by means of the Holy Spirit, Christ himself comes to do all this among us and for us. That is why it is important that children and young people receive the sacrament of confirmation.

> *Confirmation, like every sacrament, is not the work of human beings but of God, who cares for our lives as to mold us in the image of his Son, to make us capable of loving as he loves.*

Dear brothers and sisters, let us remember that we have received confirmation! All of us! Let us remember it, first in order to thank the Lord for this gift, and then to ask him to help us live as true Christians, to walk always with joy in the Holy Spirit who has been given to us.

10

The Eucharist: Sacrament of Love

General Audience, February 5, 2014

Now I would like to talk to you about the Eucharist. The Eucharist is at the heart of Christian initiation, together with baptism and confirmation, and it constitutes the source of the Church's life itself. From this sacrament of love, in fact, flows every authentic journey of faith, of communion, and of witness.

What we see when we gather to celebrate the Eucharist, the Mass, already gives us an intuition of what we are about to live. At the center of the space intended for the celebration there is an altar, which is a table covered with a tablecloth, and this makes us think of a banquet. On the table there is a cross to indicate that on this altar what is offered is the sacrifice of Christ; he is the spiritual food that we receive there, under the species of bread and wine. Beside the table is the ambo, the place from which the Word of God is proclaimed, and this indicates that there we gather to listen to the Lord, who speaks through sacred Scripture, and therefore the food that we receive is also his Word.

Word and bread in the Mass become one, as at the Last Supper, when all the words of Jesus, and all the signs he had performed, were condensed into the gesture of breaking the bread and offering the chalice, in anticipation of the sacrifice of the cross, and in these words: "Take, eat; this is my body. . . . Take, drink of it; for this is my blood."

Jesus' gesture at the Last Supper is the ultimate thanksgiving to the Father for his love, for his mercy. "Thanksgiving" in Greek is expressed as *Eucharist.*

And that is why the sacrament is called the Eucharist: it is the supreme thanksgiving to the Father, who so loved us that he gave us his Son out of love. This is why the term *Eucharist* includes the whole of that act, which is the act of God and human beings together, the act of Jesus Christ, true God and true Man.

Therefore the Eucharistic celebration is much more than a simple banquet; it is exactly the memorial of Jesus' paschal sacrifice, the mystery at the center of salvation. "Memorial" does not simply mean a remembrance, a mere memory; it means that every time we celebrate this sacrament we participate in the mystery of the passion, death, and resurrection of Christ. The Eucharist is the summit of God's saving action: the Lord Jesus, by becoming bread broken for us, pours upon us all of his mercy and his love, so as to renew our hearts, our lives, and our way of relating with him and with our brothers and sisters. It is for this reason that commonly, when we approach this sacrament, we speak of "receiving Communion," of "taking Communion." This means that by the power of the Holy Spirit, participation in Holy Communion conforms us in a singular and profound way to Christ, giving us now, already, a foretaste of the full communion with the Father that characterizes the heavenly banquet, where together with all the saints we will have the joy of contemplating God face to face.

Dear friends, we don't ever thank the Lord enough for the gift he has given us in the Eucharist! It is a very great gift, and that is why it is so important to go to Mass on Sunday. Go to Mass not just to pray, but to receive Communion, the bread that is the Body of Jesus Christ who saves us, forgives us, and unites us to the Father. It is a beautiful thing to do!

> *"Memorial" does not simply mean a remembrance; it means that every time we celebrate this sacrament we participate in the mystery of the passion, death, and resurrection of Christ.*

And we go to Mass every Sunday because that is the day of the resurrection of the Lord. That is why Sunday is so important to us. And in this Eucharist we feel this belonging to the Church, to the People of God, to the Body of God, to Jesus Christ. We will never completely grasp the value and the richness of it. Let us ask him then that this sacrament continue to keep his presence alive in the Church and to shape our community in charity and communion, according to the Father's heart. This is done throughout life but is begun on the day of our First Communion. It is important that children be prepared well for their First Communion and that every child receives it, because it is the first step of this intense belonging to Jesus Christ, after baptism and confirmation.

11

Living the Eucharist

General Audience, February 12, 2014

I have emphasized previously how the Eucharist introduces us into real communion with Jesus and his mystery. Now let us ask ourselves several questions that spring from the relationship between the Eucharist that we celebrate and our life, as a Church and as individual Christians. *How do we experience the Eucharist?* When we go to Sunday Mass, how do we live it? Is it only a moment of celebration, an established tradition, an opportunity to find oneself or to feel justified, or is it something more?

There are very specific signals for understanding how we are living the Eucharist, how we experience it. These signals tell us if we are living the Eucharist in a good way or not very well. The first indicator is our *way of looking at or considering others*. In the Eucharist, Christ is always renewing his gift of self, which he made on the cross. His whole life is an act of total sharing of self out of love; thus, he loved to be with his disciples and with the people whom he had a chance to know. For him this meant sharing in their aspirations, their problems, what stirred their souls and their lives.

Now, when participating in holy Mass, we find ourselves with all sorts of men and women: young people, the elderly, children, poor and well-off, locals and strangers alike, people with their families and people who are alone. . . . But the Eucharist I celebrate, does it lead me to truly feel that they are all like brothers and sisters? Does it increase my capacity to rejoice with those who are rejoicing and cry with those who are crying? Does it urge me to go out to the poor, the sick, the marginalized? Does it help me recognize in theirs the face of Jesus? We go to Mass because we love Jesus and we want to share, through the Eucharist, in his passion and his resurrection. But do we love, as Jesus wishes, those brothers and sisters who are the most needy?

For example, in Rome [. . .] we have seen much social discomfort either due to the rain, which has caused so much damage to entire districts, or because of the lack of work, a consequence of the global economic crisis. I wonder, and each one of us should wonder: I who go to Mass, how do I live this? Do I try to help, to approach those who are in difficulty and to pray for them? Or am I a little indifferent? Or perhaps do I just want to chat—"Did you see how this or that one is dressed?" Sometimes this happens after Mass, and it should not! We must concern ourselves with our brothers and sisters who need us because of an illness or a problem. [. . .]

A second indication that we are, or are not, living the Eucharist is a very important one: the grace of *feeling forgiven and ready to forgive*. At times someone may ask, "Why must one go to Church, given that those who regularly partici-pate in holy Mass are still sinners like the oth-ers?" We have heard it many times! In reality, the one celebrating the Eucharist doesn't do so because he believes he is, or wants to appear, bet-

> But the Eucharist I celebrate, does it increase my capacity to rejoice with those who are rejoicing and cry with those who are crying? Does it help me recognize in theirs the face of Jesus?

ter than others, but precisely because he acknowledges that he is always in need of being accepted and reborn by the mercy of God, made flesh in Jesus Christ.

If any one of us does not feel in need of the mercy of God, does not see himself as a sinner, it is better for him not to go to Mass! We go to Mass because we are sinners and we want to receive God's pardon, to participate in the redemption of Jesus, in his forgiveness. The "confession" that we make at the beginning is not "pro forma"; it is a real act of repentance! I am a sinner and I confess it, this is how the Mass begins! We should never for-get that the Last Supper of Jesus took place "on the night he was betrayed" (1 Cor. 11:23). In the bread and in the wine which we offer and around which we gather, the gift of Christ's body and blood is renewed every time for the remission of our sins. We must go to Mass humbly, like sinners, and the Lord reconciles us.

A last valuable indication comes to us from the relationship between the Eucharistic celebration and *the life of our Christian communities*. We must always bear in mind that the Eucharist is not something we make; it is not our own commemoration of what Jesus said and did. No. It is precisely an act of Christ! It is Christ who acts there, who is on the altar. It is a gift of Christ, who makes himself present and gathers us around him, to nourish us with his Word and with his life.

This means that the mission and the very identity of the Church flow from there, from the Eucharist, and there always takes its shape. A celebration may be flawless on the exterior, very beautiful, but if it does not lead us to encounter Jesus Christ, it is unlikely to bear any kind of nourishment to our heart and our life. Through the Eucharist, however, Christ wishes to enter into our life and permeate it with his grace, so that in every Christian community there may be coherence between liturgy and life.

The heart fills with trust and hope by pondering Jesus' words recounted in the Gospel: "Anyone who does eat my flesh and drink my blood has eternal life, and I shall raise that person up on the last day" (John 6:54, *NJB*). Let us live the Eucharist with the spirit of faith, of prayer, of forgiveness, of repentance, of communal joy, of concern for the needy and for the needs of so many brothers and sisters, in the certainty that the Lord will fulfill what he has promised us: eternal life.

12

Reconciliation: The Power of Forgiveness

General Audience, February 19, 2014

Through the sacraments of Christian initiation—baptism, confirmation, and the Eucharist—we receive new life in Christ. Now, we all know that we carry this life "in earthen vessels" (2 Cor. 4:7). We are still subject to temptation, suffering, and death, and because of sin, we may even lose this new life. That is why the Lord Jesus willed that the Church continue his saving work even to her own members, especially through the sacrament of reconciliation and the anointing of the sick, which can be united under the heading "sacraments of healing." The sacrament of reconciliation is a sacrament of healing. When I go to confession, it is to be healed—to heal my soul, to heal my heart, and to be healed of some wrongdoing. The biblical icon that best expresses them in their deep bond is the episode of the forgiving and healing of the paralytic, where the Lord Jesus is revealed as the physician not only of souls but also of bodies (cf. Mark 2:1–12; Matt. 9:1–8; Luke 5:17–26).

The sacrament of penance and reconciliation flows directly from the paschal mystery. In fact, on the evening of Easter, the Lord appeared to the disciples, who were locked in the Upper Room, and after addressing them with the greeting, "Peace be with you!" he breathed on them and said, "Receive the Holy Spirit. If you forgive the sins of any, they are forgiven" (John 20:21–23). This passage reveals to us the most profound dynamic contained in this sacrament.

First, Jesus' words reveal that the forgiveness of our sins is not something we can give ourselves. I cannot say, "I forgive my sins." Forgiveness is asked for, is asked of another, and in confession we ask for forgiveness from Jesus. Forgiveness is not the fruit of our own efforts but rather it's a gift; it is a gift of the Holy Spirit, who fills us with the wellspring of mercy and of grace that flows unceasingly from the open heart of the crucified and risen Christ.

Second, Jesus reminds us that we can truly be at peace only if we allow ourselves to be reconciled, in the Lord Jesus, with the Father and with one another. And we have all felt this in our hearts, when we have gone to confession with a soul weighed down and with a little sadness; when we receive Jesus' forgiveness we feel at peace, with that peace of soul which is so beautiful, and which only Jesus can give.

Over time, the celebration of this sacrament of reconciliation has passed from a public form—because at first it was made publicly—to a personal one, to the confidential form of confession. This, however, does not entail losing the ecclesial matrix that constitutes its vital context. In fact, the Christian community is the place where the Spirit is made present, who renews hearts in the love of God and makes us all one in Christ Jesus.

That is why it is not enough to ask the Lord for forgiveness in one's own mind and heart, but why instead it is necessary humbly and trustingly to confess one's sins to a minister of the Church. In the celebration of this sacrament, the priest represents not only God but also the whole community, who sees itself in the weakness of each of its members, who listens and is moved by that person's repentance, and who is reconciled with him, who cheers him up and accompanies him on the path of conversion and of human and Christian growth.

One might say, "I confess only to God." Yes, you can say to God, "Forgive me" and name your sins, but our sins are also committed against the fellowship and against the Church. That is why it is necessary to ask pardon of the Church, and of brothers and sisters in the person of the priest. [You may say,] "But Father, I am ashamed.". . . Shame is also good; it is healthy to feel a little shame, because being ashamed is salutary. In my country, when a person feels no shame, we say that he is "shameless," a "sin *verguenza*." But shame [can bring a good effect] because it makes us more humble, and the priest receives this confession with love and tenderness and forgives us on God's behalf.

Also from a human point of view, in order to unburden oneself, it is good to talk with a brother and tell the priest these things that are weighing so much on one's heart. And one feels that one is unburdening oneself before God, with the Church, with his brother. Do not be afraid of confession! When one is in line to go to

> *Yes, you can say to God, "Forgive me" and name your sins, but our sins are also committed against the fellowship and against the Church.*

confession, one feels all these things, even shame, but then when one finishes confession, one leaves free, grand, beautiful, forgiven, candid, happy. This is the beauty of confession! I would like to ask you [. . .]: when was the last time you made your confession? [. . .] Two days, two weeks, two years, twenty years, forty years? [. . .] And if much time has passed, do not lose another day. Go, the priest will be good. Jesus is there, and Jesus is more benevolent than priests; Jesus receives you, he receives you with so much love. Be courageous and go to confession!

Dear friends, celebrating the sacrament of reconciliation means being enfolded in a warm embrace: it is the embrace of the Father's infinite mercy. Let us recall that beautiful, beautiful parable of the son who left his home with the money of his inheritance. He wasted all the money and then, when he had nothing left, he decided to return home, not as a son but as a servant. His heart was filled with so much guilt and shame. The surprise came when he began to speak, to ask for forgiveness. His father did not let him speak—he embraced him, he kissed him, and he began to make merry. But I am telling you: each time we go to confession, God embraces us. God rejoices! Let us go forward on this road.

13

Anointing of the Sick: God's Compassion as We Persevere

General Audience, February 26, 2014

Now I would like to talk to you about the sacrament of the anointing of the sick, which allows us to touch God's compassion for humanity. In the past it was called "extreme unction" because it was understood as a spiritual comfort in the face of imminent death. To speak instead of the "anointing of the sick" helps us broaden our vision to include the experience of illness and suffering, within the horizon of God's mercy.

There is a biblical icon that expresses, in all its depths, the mystery that shines through the anointing of the sick. It is the parable of the Good Samaritan contained in the Gospel of Luke (10:30–35). Each time we celebrate this sacrament, the Lord Jesus, in the person of the priest, comes close to the one who suffers, who is elderly or seriously ill. The parable says that the Good Samaritan takes care of the suffering man by pouring oil and wine on his wounds. Oil makes us think of that which is blessed by the bishop each year at the Holy Thursday Chrism Mass, precisely in view of the anointing of the sick. Wine, however, is a sign of Christ's love and grace, which flow from the gift of his life for us and are expressed in all their richness in the sacramental life of the Church. Finally, the suffering person is entrusted to an innkeeper, so that he might continue to care for him, sparing no expense. Now, who is this innkeeper? It is the Church, the Christian community—it is us—to whom each day the Lord entrusts those who are afflicted in body and spirit, so that we might lavish all of his mercy and salvation upon them without measure.

This mandate is repeated in an explicit and precise manner in the Letter of James, where he recommends: "Any one of you who is ill should send for the elders of the church, and they must anoint the sick person with oil in the name of the Lord and pray over him. The prayer of faith will save the sick person and the Lord will raise him up again; and if he has committed any sins, he will be forgiven" (5:14–15, *NJB*). It was therefore a practice that was already taking place at the time of the apostles.

Jesus in fact taught his disciples to have the same preferential love that he did for the sick and suffering, and he transmitted to them the ability and duty to continue providing, in his name and after his own heart, relief and peace through the special grace of this sacrament. This, however, should not make us fall into an obsessive search for miracles or the presumption that one can always and in any situation be healed. Rather, it is the reassurance of Jesus' closeness to the sick and to the aged, too, because any elderly person, anyone over the age of sixty-five, can receive this sacrament, through which Jesus himself draws close to us.

But when someone is sick, and we say, "Let's call for the priest to come," sometimes we think, *No, then he will bring bad luck, let's not call him,* or *He will scare the sick person.* Why do we think this? Because the idea is floating about that the undertakers arrive after the priest. And this is not true. The priest comes to help the sick or elderly person; that is why the priest's visit to the sick is so important. We ought to call the priest

> *The priest and those who are present during the anointing of the sick represent the entire Christian community that as one body huddles around the one who suffers and also around her family.*

to the sick person's side and say, "Come, give him the anointing, bless him." It is Jesus himself who comes to relieve the sick person, to give him strength, to give him hope, to help him, and also to forgive his sins. And this is very beautiful!

And we must not think that this is taboo, because in times of pain and illness it is always good to know that we are not alone. The priest and those who are present during the anointing of the sick, in fact, represent the entire Christian community that as one body huddles around the one who suffers and also around her family, nurturing their faith and hope, and supporting them through their prayers and fraternal warmth. But the greatest comfort comes from the fact that it is the Lord Jesus who makes himself present in the sacrament, who takes us by the hand, who caresses us as he did with the sick, and who reminds us that we already belong to him and that nothing—not even evil and death—can ever separate us from him.

14

Religious Vocations:
Walking in Service

General Audience, March 26, 2014

We have already had occasion to point out that the three sacraments of baptism, confirmation, and the Eucharist together constitute the mystery of Christian initiation, a single great event of grace that regenerates us in Christ. This is the fundamental vocation that unites everyone in the Church as disciples of the Lord Jesus. There are then two sacraments that correspond to two specific vocations: holy orders and matrimony. They constitute two great paths by which the Christian can make his or her life a gift of love, after the example and in the name of Christ, and thus cooperate in the building up of the Church.

Holy orders, in its three grades of bishop, priest, and deacon, is the sacrament that enables a man to exercise the ministry that the Lord Jesus entrusted to the apostles, to shepherd his flock, in the power of his Spirit and according to his heart. [Those in holy orders] tend Jesus' flock not by the power of human strength or by their own power, but by the Spirit's and according to his heart, the heart of Jesus, which is a heart of love. The priest, the bishop, and the deacon must shepherd the Lord's flock with love. It is useless if it is not done with love. And in this sense, the ministers who are chosen and consecrated for this service extend Jesus' presence in time, if they do so by the power of the Holy Spirit, in God's name and with love.

A first aspect of holy orders is that those who are ordained are placed *at the head of the community*. They are "at the head," yes, but for Jesus this means placing one's authority *at the service* [of the community], as Jesus himself showed and taught his disciples with these words: "You know that the rulers of the Gentiles lord it over

> *Through holy orders the minister dedicates himself entirely to his community and loves it with all his heart: it is his family.*

them, and their great men exercise authority over them. It shall not be so among you; but whoever would be great among you must be your servant, and whoever would be first among you must be your slave; even as the Son of man came not to be served but to serve, and to give his life as a ransom for many" (Matt. 20:25–28; Mark 10:42–45). A bishop who is not at the service of the community fails to perform his duty; a priest who is not at the service of his community fails to perform his duty, he errs.

Another aspect of holy orders, one that grows out of this sacramental union with Christ, is *a passionate love for the Church*. Let us think of that passage from the Letter to the Ephesians in which St. Paul states that Christ "loved the Church and gave himself up for her, that he might sanctify her, having cleansed her by the washing of water with the word, that he might present the Church to himself in splendor, without spot or wrinkle or any such thing" (5:25–27). Through holy orders the minister dedicates himself entirely to his community and loves it with all his heart: it is his family. The bishop and the priest love the Church in their own community, they love it greatly. How? As Christ loves the Church. St. Paul will say the same of marriage: the husband is to love his wife as Christ loves the Church. It is a great mystery of love: priesthood and matrimony are two sacraments, pathways people normally take to go to the Lord.

A final aspect of holy orders is reflected in what the apostle Paul recommends to the disciple Timothy—that he not neglect, indeed that he always *rekindle, the gift that is within him*. This is the gift he has been given through the laying on of hands (cf. 1 Tim. 4:14; 2 Tim. 1:6). When the ministry is not fostered—the ministry of the bishop, the ministry of the priest—through prayer, through listening to the Word of God, through the daily celebration of the Eucharist, and also through regularly going to the sacrament of penance, he inevitably loses sight of the authentic meaning of his own service and the joy that comes from a profound communion with Jesus.

The bishop who does not pray, the bishop who does not listen to the Word of God, who does not celebrate every day, who does not regularly confess—and the same is true for the priest who does not do these things—in the long run loses his union with Jesus and becomes so mediocre that he does not benefit the Church. That is why we must help bishops and priests to pray, to listen to the Word of God, which is one's daily nourishment, to celebrate the Eucharist each day, and to confess regularly. This is so important precisely because it concerns the sanctification of bishops and priests.

I would like to conclude with this: how does one become a priest? Where is access to the priesthood sold? No, it is not sold. This is an initiative that the Lord takes. The Lord calls. He calls each of those whom he wills to become priests. Perhaps there are some young men present here who have heard this call in their hearts, the aspiration to become a priest, the desire to serve others in the things of God, the desire to spend one's entire life in service in order to catechize, baptize, forgive, celebrate the Eucharist, heal the sick . . . the whole of one's life spent in this way. If some of you have heard this call in your heart, it is Jesus who has placed it there. Pay attention to this invitation and pray that it might grow and bear fruit for the whole Church.

15

Christian Marriage: Walking in Covenant

General Audience, April 2, 2014

Let us conclude the series of catechesis on the sacraments by speaking about matrimony. This sacrament leads us to the heart of God's design, which is a plan for a covenant with his people, with us all, a plan for communion. At the beginning of the book of Genesis, the first book of the Bible, at the culmination of the creation account it says: "God created man in his own image, in the image of God he created him; male and female he created them. . . . Therefore a man leaves his father and his mother and cleaves to his wife, and they become one flesh" (Gen. 1:27; 2:24). The image of God is the married couple: the man and the woman—not only the man, not only the woman, but both of them together. This is the image of God: love. God's covenant with us is represented in that covenant between man and woman. And this is very beautiful! We are created in order to love, as a reflection of God and his love. And in the marital union man and woman fulfill this vocation through their mutual reciprocity and their full and definitive communion of life.

When a man and a woman celebrate the sacrament of matrimony, God, as it were, is "mirrored" in them; he impresses in them his own features and the indelible character of his love. Marriage is the icon of God's love for us. Indeed, God is communion too: the three Persons of the Father, the Son, and the Holy Spirit live eternally in perfect unity. And this is precisely the mystery of matrimony: God makes of the two spouses one single life. The

Bible uses a powerful expression and says "one flesh," so intimate is the union between a man and a woman in marriage. And this is precisely the mystery of marriage: the love of God that is reflected in the couple that decides to live together. Therefore a man leaves his home, the home of his parents, and goes to live with his wife and unites himself so strongly to her that the two become—the Bible says—one flesh.

St. Paul, in the Letter to the Ephesians, emphasizes that a great mystery is reflected in Christian spouses: the relationship established by Christ with the Church, a nuptial relationship (cf. Eph. 5:21–33). The Church is the Bride of Christ. This is their relationship. This means that matrimony responds to a specific vocation and must be considered as a consecration (cf. *Gaudium et Spes*, n. 48: *Familiaris Consortio*, n. 56). It is a consecration; the man and woman are consecrated in their love. The spouses, in fact, in virtue of the sacrament, are invested with a true and proper mission, so that starting with the simple ordinary things of life they may make visible the love with which Christ loves his Church, by continuing to give his life for her in fidelity and service.

> *When a man and a woman celebrate the sacrament of matrimony, God, as it were, is "mirrored" in them; he impresses in them his own features and the indelible character of his love.*

There is a truly marvelous design inherent in the sacrament of matrimony! And it unfolds in the simplicity and frailty of the human condition. We are well aware of how many difficulties two spouses experience. . . . The important thing is to keep alive their bond with God, who stands as the foundation of the marital bond. And the true bond is always the Lord. When the family prays, the bond is preserved. When the husband prays for his wife and the wife prays for her husband, that bond becomes strong; one praying for the other.

It is true that there are so many difficulties in married life, so many, when there is insufficient work or money, when the children have problems—so much to contend with. And many times the husband and wife become a little fractious and argue between themselves. They argue, this is how it is, there is always arguing in marriage, sometimes the plates even fly. Yet we must not become saddened by this; it is the human condition. The secret is that love is stronger than the moment when there is arguing, and therefore I always advise spouses: do not let a day when you have argued end without making peace. Always! And to make peace it isn't necessary to call the United Nations to come to the house and make peace. A little gesture is sufficient, a caress, and then let it be! Until tomorrow! And tomorrow begin again. And this is life, carrying on, carrying on with courage and the desire to live together. And this is truly great, it is beautiful! Married life is such a beautiful thing, and we must treasure it always, and treasure the children.

On other occasions [. . .] I have mentioned something else that is so helpful for marriage. There are three [phrases] that always need to be said [. . .] at home: *may I, thank you,* and *sorry*. The three magic [phrases]. *May I*: so as not to be intrusive. May I, but how does it seem to you? May I, please allow me. *Thank you*: to thank one's spouse; thank you for what you did for me, thank you for this. That beauty of giving thanks! And since we all make mistakes, that other word which is a bit hard to say but which needs to be said: *Sorry*. Please, thank you, and sorry. With these [. . .] words, with the prayer of the husband for the wife and vice versa, by always making peace before the day comes to an end, [they will help their] marriage go forward.

PART THREE

The Gifts of the Walk

16

Holy Spirit: Our Companion on the Way

Homily, June 8, 2014

"They were all filled with the Holy Spirit" (Acts 2:4).

Speaking to the apostles at the Last Supper, Jesus said that after he left this world he would send them *the gift of the Father*, that is, the Holy Spirit (cf. John 15:26). This promise was powerfully fulfilled on the day of Pentecost, when the Holy Spirit descended upon the disciples, who were gathered in the Upper Room. This extraordinary outpouring was not limited solely to that moment but was an event that was renewed and still continues to be renewed. Christ glorified at the right hand of the Father continues to fulfill his promise, sending upon the Church the life-giving Spirit, who *teaches us, reminds us,* and *lets us speak.*

The Holy Spirit *teaches us*; he is the Interior Master. He guides us along the right path, through life's challenges. He teaches us the path, the way. In the early times of the Church, Christianity was called "the way" (cf. Acts 9:2), and Jesus himself is the Way. The Holy Spirit teaches us to follow him, to walk in his footprints. More than a master of doctrine, the Holy Spirit is a master of life. And he surely takes part in life as well as in knowledge, but within the broadest and most harmonious horizons of Christian existence.

The Holy Spirit *reminds us*; he reminds us of all that Jesus said. He is the living memory of the Church, and when he reminds us, he helps us understand the words of the Lord.

This remembrance in the Spirit and by virtue of the Spirit is not reduced to a mnemonic fact; it is an essential aspect of Christ's presence within us and within his Church. The Spirit of truth and charity reminds us of all that Christ said and helps us enter ever more fully into the meaning of his words. We all have this experi-

> *Jesus himself is the Way. The Holy Spirit teaches us to follow him, to walk in his footprints. More than a master of doctrine, the Holy Spirit is a master of life.*

ence: one moment, in any situation, there is an idea and then another connects with a passage from Scripture. . . . It is the Spirit who leads us to take this path: the path of the living memory of the Church. And he asks us for a response: the more generous our response, the more Jesus' words become life within us, becoming attitudes, choices, actions, testimony. In essence the Spirit reminds us of the commandment of love and calls us to live it.

A Christian without memory is not a true Christian but only halfway there: a man or a woman, a prisoner of the moment, who doesn't know how to treasure his or her history, doesn't know how to read it and live it as salvation history. With the help of the Holy Spirit, however, we are able to interpret interior inspirations and life events in light of Jesus' words. And thus within us grows the knowledge of memory, knowledge of the heart, which is a gift of the Spirit. May the Holy Spirit rekindle the Christian memory within all of us! And there, that day with the apostles, was Our Lady of Memory, who from the beginning meditated on all those things in her heart. Mary, our Mother, was there. May she help us on this path of memory.

The Holy Spirit teaches us, reminds us, and—another aspect—*lets us speak*, with God and with our fellow human beings. There are no muted Christians, mute of soul—no, there's no place for this.

He lets us speak with God in *prayer*. Prayer is a gift that we freely receive; dialoguing with him in the Holy Spirit, who prays in us and allows us to address God, calling him Father, Dad, *Abba* (cf. Rom. 8:15; Gal. 4:4); and this is not merely an expression but a reality: we *truly* are children of God. "All who are led by the Spirit of God are children of God" (Rom. 8:14).

He lets us speak in the act of faith. Without the Holy Spirit, none of us is able to say, "Jesus is Lord." It is the Spirit who lets us speak with people in *fraternal dialogue.* He lets us speak with others, recognizing them as brothers and sisters; to speak with friendship, with tenderness, with compassion, understanding the heartaches and hopes, the sorrows and joys of others.

But there's more: the Holy Spirit also lets us speak to men and women through *prophecy*, making us humble and docile channels of God's Word. Prophecy is made with candor, to openly demonstrate the contradictions and injustices, but always with compassion and constructive intent. Charged with the Spirit of love, we can be signs and instruments of God, who loves, who serves, who gives life.

In summary: the Holy Spirit teaches us the way; he reminds us of and explains Jesus' words; he lets us pray and say "Father" to God; he lets us speak to men and women in fraternal dialogue; and he lets us speak in prophecy.

The day of Pentecost, when the disciples "were all filled with the Holy Spirit," was the baptism of the Church, which was born in "going out," in departure, to proclaim the Good News to everyone. The Mother Church departs in order to serve. Let us remember the other Mother, our Mother who sets out in haste to serve. Mother Church and Mother Mary: both virgins, both mothers, both women. Jesus was peremptory with the apostles: do not depart from Jerusalem, but wait until you have received the power of the Holy Spirit from above (cf. Acts 1:4–8). Without him there is no mission, there is no evangelization. For this, with the whole Church, with our Mother Catholic Church, let us implore: Come, Holy Spirit!

17

Walking with Wisdom

General Audience, April 9, 2014

The Spirit himself is "the gift of God" par excellence (cf. John 4:10). He is a gift of God, and he in turn communicates various spiritual gifts to those who receive him. The Church identifies *seven*, a number that symbolically speaks of *fullness, completeness*; these gifts are those we learn about when we prepare for the sacrament of confirmation and which we invoke in the ancient prayer called the "Sequence of the Holy Spirit." The gifts of the Holy Spirit are *wisdom, understanding, counsel, fortitude, knowledge, piety*, and *fear of the Lord*.

The first gift of the Holy Spirit according to this list is therefore *wisdom*. But it is not simply human wisdom, which is the fruit of knowledge and experience. In the Bible we are told that Solomon, at the time of his coronation as king of Israel, had asked for the gift of wisdom (cf. 1 Kings 3:9). And wisdom is precisely this: it is the grace of being able to *see everything with the eyes of God*. It is simply this: it is to see the world, to see situations, circumstances, problems, everything through God's eyes. [. . .] Sometimes we see things according to our liking or according to the condition of our heart, with love or with hate, with envy. . . . No, this is not God's perspective. Wisdom is what the Holy Spirit works in us so as to enable us to see things with the eyes of God. This is the gift of wisdom.

And obviously this comes from *intimacy with God*, from the intimate relationship we have with God, from the relationship children have with their Father. And when we have this relationship, the Holy Spirit endows us with the gift of wisdom. When we are in communion with the Lord, the Holy Spirit transfigures our heart and enables it to perceive all of his warmth and predilection.

> *And wisdom is precisely this: to see the world, to see situations, circumstances, problems, everything through God's eyes.*

The Holy Spirit thus makes a Christian "wise," not in the sense of having an answer for everything, but in the sense that one *"knows" about God*. Christians with this wisdom know how God acts, know when something is of God and when it is not of God; they have this wisdom that God places in their hearts. The hearts of the wise in this sense have a *taste and savor for God*. And how important it is that there be Christians like this in our communities! Everything in them speaks of God and becomes a beautiful and living sign of his presence and of his love. And this is something that we cannot invent, that we cannot obtain by ourselves; it is a gift that God gives to those who make themselves docile to the Holy Spirit. We have the Holy Spirit within us, in our hearts; we can listen to him. . . . If we listen to the Holy Spirit, he teaches us this way of wisdom, he endows us with wisdom, which is seeing with God's eyes, hearing with God's ears, loving with God's heart, directing things with God's judgment. This is the wisdom the Holy Spirit endows us with, and we can all have it. We only have to ask it of the Holy Spirit.

Think of a mother at her home with the children; when one child does something, the other thinks of something else, and the poor mother goes to and fro with the problems of her children. And when mothers get tired and scold the children, is that wisdom? Scolding children—is this wisdom? What do you say: is it wisdom or not? No! Instead, when the mother takes her child aside and gently reproves him, saying, "Don't do this, because . . ." and explains with great patience, is this the wisdom of God? Yes! It is what the Holy Spirit gives us in life!

Then, in marriage, for example, the two spouses argue, and then they don't look at each other, or if they do look at each other, they look at each other with displeasure: is this the wisdom of God? No! Instead, if one says, "Ah well, the storm has passed, let's make peace," and they begin again and go forward in peace: is this wisdom? [. . .] [T]his is the gift of wisdom. May it come to our homes; may we have it with the children; may it come to us all!

And this cannot be learned; this is a gift of the Holy Spirit. Therefore, we must ask the Lord to grant us the Holy Spirit and to grant us the gift of *wisdom*, that *wisdom of God* that teaches us to see with God's eyes, to feel with God's heart, to speak with God's words. And so, with this wisdom, let us go forward, let us build our family, let us build the Church, and we will all be sanctified. Today let us ask for this grace of wisdom. And let us ask Our Lady, who is the Seat of Wisdom, for this gift. May she give us this grace.

18

Walking with Understanding

General Audience, April 30, 2014

Having considered wisdom as the first of the seven gifts of the Holy Spirit, now I would like to focus on the second gift, which is *understanding*. We are not dealing here with human understanding, with the intellectual prowess with which we may be more or less endowed. Rather, it is a grace that only the Holy Spirit can infuse and that awakens in a Christian the ability to go beyond the outward appearance of reality and *to probe the depths of the thoughts of God and his plan of salvation.*

The apostle Paul, addressing the community at Corinth, aptly describes the effects of this gift—that is, what the gift of understanding does in us—and Paul says this: "What no eye has seen, nor ear heard, nor the heart of man conceived, what God has prepared for those who love him, God has revealed to us through the Spirit" (1 Cor. 2:9–10). This of course does not mean that a Christian can comprehend all things and have full knowledge of the designs of God; all of this waits to be revealed in all its clarity once we stand in the sight of God and are truly one with him. However, as the very word suggests, understanding allows us to *intus legere*, or "to read inwardly." This gift enables us to understand things as God understands them, with the mind of God. For one can understand a situation with human understanding, with prudence, and this is good. But to understand a situation in depth, as God understands it, is the effect of this gift. And Jesus desired to send us the Holy Spirit so that we might have this gift, so that all of us might understand things as God understands them, with the mind of God. What a beautiful gift the Lord has given us. It is the gift with which the Holy Spirit introduces us into intimacy with God and makes us sharers in the plan of love that he has for us.

It is clear then that the gift of understanding is *closely connected to faith*. When the *Holy Spirit* dwells in our hearts and enlightens our minds, he makes us grow day by day in the *understanding of what the Lord has said and accomplished*. Jesus himself told his disciples, "I will send you the Holy Spirit, and he will enable you to understand all that I have taught you," meaning, to understand the teachings of Jesus, to understand his Word, to understand the Gospel, to understand the Word of God. One can read the Gospel and understand something, but if we read the Gospel with this gift of the Holy Spirit, we can understand the depths of God's words. And this is a great gift, a great gift for which we all must ask, and ask together: Give us, Lord, the gift of understanding.

There is an episode in the Gospel of Luke that aptly expresses the depths and power of this gift. After witnessing the death on the cross and the burial of Jesus, two of his disciples, disappointed and grief stricken, leave Jerusalem and return to their village called Emmaus. As they are on their way, the risen Jesus draws near and begins talking with them, but their eyes, veiled with sadness and despair, are unable to recognize him. Jesus walks with them, but they are so sad, in such deep despair, that they do not recognize him.

> When the Holy Spirit dwells in our hearts and enlightens our minds, he makes us grow day by day in the understanding of what Jesus has said and accomplished.

When, however, the Lord explains the Scriptures to them so that they might understand that he had to suffer and die in order then to rise again, *their minds are opened and hope is rekindled in their hearts* (cf. Luke 24:13–27). And this is what the Holy Spirit does with us: he opens our minds, he opens us to understand better the things of God—human things, situations, all things. The gift of understanding is important for our Christian life. Let us ask it of the Lord, that he may give us all this gift to understand the things that happen as he understands them, and to understand, above all, the Word of God in the Gospel.

19

Walking with Good Counsel

General Audience, May 7, 2014

We read in the book of Psalms, "the Lord who gives me counsel; in the night also my heart instructs me" (Ps. 16[15]:7). This is another gift of the Holy Spirit: the gift of *counsel*. We know how important it is in the most delicate moments to be able to count on the advice of people who are wise and who love us. Now, through the gift of counsel, it is God himself, through his Spirit, who enlightens our hearts so as to make us understand the right way to speak and to behave and the way to follow. But how does this gift work in us?

When we receive and welcome him into our heart, the Holy Spirit immediately begins to make us sensitive to his voice and to guide our thoughts, our feelings, and our intentions according to the heart of God. At the same time, he leads us more and more to turn our interior gaze to Jesus, as the model of our way of acting and of relating with God the Father and with our brothers and sisters. Counsel, then, is the gift through which the Holy Spirit *enables our conscience to make a concrete choice in communion with God*, according to the logic of Jesus and his Gospel. In this way, the Spirit makes us grow interiorly; he makes us grow positively; he makes us grow in the community; and he helps us not to fall prey to self-centeredness and our own way of seeing things. Thus the Spirit helps us to grow and also to live in community.

The essential condition for preserving this gift is prayer. We always return to the same theme: prayer! Yet prayer is so important. To pray with the prayers that we all learned as children, but also to pray in our own words. To ask, "Lord, help me, give me counsel, what must I do now?" And through prayer we make space so that the Spirit may come and help us in that moment, that he may counsel us on what we all

> When we receive and welcome him into our heart, the Holy Spirit immediately begins to make us sensitive to his voice and to guide our thoughts, feelings, and intentions according to the heart of God.

must do. Prayer! Never forget prayer. Never! No one realizes when we pray on the bus, on the road: we pray in the silence of our heart. Let us take advantage of these moments to pray, and pray that the Spirit give us the gift of counsel.

In intimacy with God and in listening to his Word, little by little we put aside our own way of thinking, which is most often dictated by our tunnel vision, by our prejudice, and by our ambitions, and we learn instead to ask the Lord, What is your desire? What is your will? What pleases you? In this way a deep, almost *connatural harmony* in the Spirit grows and develops within us, and we experience how true the words of Jesus are that are reported in the Gospel of Matthew: "Do not be anxious how you are to speak or what you are to say; for what you are to say will be given to you in that hour; for it is not you who speak, but the Spirit of your Father speaking through you" (Matt. 10:19–20).

It is the Spirit who counsels us, but we have to make room for the Spirit, so that he may counsel us. And to give space is to pray, to pray that he come and help us always.

As with all the other gifts of the Holy Spirit, then, counsel constitutes a treasure *for the whole Christian community*. The Lord speaks to us not only in the intimacy of the heart—yes, he speaks to us, but not only there—but also through the voice and witness of our brothers and sisters. It is truly a great gift to be able to meet men and women of faith who, especially in the most complicated and important stages of our lives, help us bring light to our heart and recognize the Lord's will!

I remember once when I was at the Shrine of Luján and I was in the confessional, where there was a long line. There was even a very modern young man, with earrings, tattoos, all these things. . . . And he came to tell me what was happening to him. It was a big and difficult problem. And he said to me, "I told my mother all this, and my mother said to me, 'Go to Our Lady, and she will tell you what you must do.'" Here is a woman who had the gift of counsel. She did not know how to help her son out of his problem, but she indicated the right road: go to Our Lady, and she will tell you. This is the gift of counsel. That humble, simple woman gave her son the truest counsel. In fact, this young man said to me, "I looked at Our Lady, and I felt that I had to do this, this, and this . . ." I did not have to speak; his mother and the boy himself had already said everything. This is the gift of counsel. You mothers who have this gift, ask it for your children. The ability to give good counsel to your children is a gift of God.

Dear friends, Psalm 16 [. . .] invites us to pray with these words: "I bless the Lord who gives me counsel; in the night also my heart instructs me. I keep the Lord always before me; because he is at my right hand, I shall not be moved" (vv. 7–8). May the Spirit always pour this certainty into our hearts and fill us thus with the consolation of his peace! Always ask for the gift of counsel.

20

Walking with Fortitude

General Audience, May 14, 2014

We reflected on the first three gifts of the Holy Spirit: wisdom, understanding, and counsel. Today let us consider what the Lord does: he always comes *to sustain us in our weakness*, and he does this by a special gift: *fortitude*.

There is a parable told by Jesus that helps us grasp the importance of this gift. A sower goes out to sow; however, not all the seed bears fruit. What falls along the path is eaten by birds; what falls on rocky ground or among brambles springs up but is soon scorched by the sun or choked by thorns. Only what falls on good soil is able to grow and bear fruit (cf. Mark 4:3–9; Matt. 13:3–9; Luke 8:4–8). As Jesus explains to his disciples, this sower represents the Father, who abundantly sows the seed of his Word. The seed, however, often meets with the aridity of our hearts and even when received is likely to remain barren. However, through the gift of fortitude, the Holy Spirit *liberates the soil of our heart*; he frees it from sluggishness, from uncertainty, and from all the fears that can hinder it, so that the Lord's Word may be put into practice authentically and with joy. The gift of fortitude is a true help; it gives us strength, and it also frees us from so many obstacles.

There are also *difficult moments* and *extreme situations* in which the gift of fortitude manifests itself in an extraordinary, exemplary way. This is the case with those who are facing particularly harsh and painful situations that disrupt their lives and those of their loved ones. The Church shines with the testimony of so many *brothers and sisters who have not hesitated to give their very lives* in order to remain faithful to the Lord and his Gospel. Even today there is no shortage of Christians who in many parts of the world continue to celebrate and bear witness to their faith with deep conviction and serenity, and who persist even when they know that this may involve them in paying a higher price.

We, too, all of us, know people who have experienced difficult situations and great suffering. Let us think of those men and women who have difficult lives, who fight to feed their families, to educate their children; they do all this because the spirit of fortitude is helping them. How many men and women there are—we do

> *The gift of fortitude is what enables [people] to carry on with their duties as individuals, fathers, mothers, brothers, sisters, citizens.*

not know their names—who honor our people, who honor our Church, because they are strong, strong in carrying forward their lives, their families, their work, their faith. These brothers and sisters of ours are saints, everyday saints, hidden saints among us. The gift of fortitude is what enables them to carry on with their duties as individuals, fathers, mothers, brothers, sisters, citizens. We have many of them! Let us thank the Lord for these Christians who live in hidden holiness; the Holy Spirit is within them carrying them forward! And it will benefit us to think about these people: *If they do all this, if they can do it, why can't I?* And it will also do us good to ask the Lord to give us the gift of fortitude.

We need not think that the gift of fortitude is necessary only on some occasions or in particular situations. This gift must constitute the tenor of our Christian life, in the *ordinary daily routine*. As I said, we need to be strong every day of our lives, to carry forward our life, our family, our faith. The apostle Paul said something that will benefit us to hear: "I can do all things through him who strengthens me" (Phil. 4:13). When we face daily life, when difficulties arise, let us remember this: "I can do all things through him who strengthens me." The Lord always strengthens us; he never lets strength lack. The Lord does not try us beyond our possibilities. He is always with us. "I can do all things through him who strengthens me."

Dear friends, sometimes we may be tempted to give in to laziness or, worse, to discouragement, especially when faced with the hardships and trials of life. In these cases, let us not lose heart. Let us invoke the Holy Spirit so that through the gift of fortitude he may lift our heart and communicate new strength and enthusiasm to our life and to our following of Jesus.

21

Walking with Knowledge

General Audience, May 21, 2014

I would like to highlight another gift of the Holy Spirit: *knowledge.* When we speak of knowledge, we immediately think of the human capacity to learn more and more about the reality that surrounds us and to discover the laws that regulate nature and the universe. The knowledge that comes from the Holy Spirit, however, is not limited to human knowledge; it is a special gift that leads us to grasp, through creation, the greatness and love of God and his profound relationship with every creature.

When our eyes are illumined by the Spirit, they open to contemplate God in the beauty of nature and in the grandeur of the cosmos, and they lead us *to discover how everything speaks to us about him and his love.* All of this arouses in us great wonder and a profound sense of gratitude! It is the sensation we experience when we admire a work of art or any marvel whatsoever that is born of human genius and creativity. Before all this, the Spirit leads us to praise the Lord from the depths of our hearts and to recognize, in all that we have and all that we are, an invaluable gift of God and a sign of his infinite love for us.

In the first chapter of Genesis, right at the beginning of the Bible, what is emphasized is that God is pleased with his creation, stressing repeatedly the beauty and goodness of every single thing. At the end of each day it is written, "God saw that it was good" (Gen. 1:10, 12, 18, 21, 25). If God sees creation as good, as a beautiful thing, then we, too, must take this attitude and see that creation is a good and beautiful thing.

Now, this is the gift of knowledge that allows us to see this beauty; therefore, we praise God, giving thanks to him for having granted us so much beauty. And when God finished creating man and woman, he didn't say "he saw that this was good" but said that this was "very good" (v. 31). In the eyes of God we are the most beautiful thing, the greatest, the best of creation; even the angels are beneath us; we are more than the angels, as we heard in the book of Psalms. The Lord favors us! We must give thanks to him for this.

The gift of knowledge sets us in profound *harmony with the Creator* and allows us to participate in the clarity of his vision and his judgment. And it is in this perspective that we manage to accept man and woman as the summit of creation, as the fulfillment of a plan of love that is impressed in each one of us and that allows us to recognize one another as brothers and sisters.

> When our eyes are illumined by the Spirit, they open to contemplate God in the beauty of nature and in the grandeur of the cosmos, and they lead us to discover how everything speaks to us about him and his love.

All this is a source of serenity and peace and makes the Christian a joyful witness of God, in the footsteps of St. Francis of Assisi and so many saints who knew how to praise and laud his love through the contemplation of creation. At the same time, however, the gift of knowledge helps us not to fall into attitudes of excess or error. The first lies in the risk of considering ourselves the masters of creation. Creation is not some possession that we can lord over for our own pleasure. Nor, even less, is it the property of only some people, the few. Creation is a gift, it is the marvelous gift that God has given us so that *we will take care of it and harness it for the benefit of all, always with great respect and gratitude.* The second erroneous attitude is [to look to creation to provide the answer to all our expectations]. With the gift of knowledge, the Spirit helps us not to fall into this error.

But I would like to return to the first of these incorrect paths: tyranny over rather than the custody of creation. We must protect creation for it is a gift the Lord has given us; it is God's present to us; we are the guardians of creation. When we exploit creation, we destroy that sign of God's love. To destroy creation is to say to God, "I don't care." And this is not good; this is sin.

Custody of creation is precisely custody of God's gift, and it is saying to God, "Thank you. I am the guardian of creation so as to make it progress, never to destroy your gift." This must be our attitude toward creation: guard it—for if we destroy creation, creation will destroy us! Don't forget that. Once I was in the countryside, and I heard a saying from a simple person who had a great love for flowers and took care of them. He said to me, "We must take care of the beautiful things that God has given us! Creation is ours so that we can receive good things from it; not to exploit it but to protect it. *God forgives always, we men forgive sometimes, but creation never forgives, and if you don't care for it, it will destroy you.*"

This should make us think and should make us ask the Holy Spirit for the gift of knowledge in order to understand better that creation is a most beautiful gift of God. He has done many good things for the thing that is most good: the human person.

22

Walking with True Piety

General Audience, June 4, 2014

We would like to dwell on a gift of the Holy Spirit that often becomes misconstrued or treated superficially but rather touches the very heart of our Christian life and identity: it is the gift of *piety*.

It should be clarified immediately that this gift is not to be identified with having compassion for someone, feeling pity on one's neighbor; rather, it indicates our belonging to God and our profound relationship with him, a bond that gives meaning to our life and keeps us sound, in communion with him, even during the most difficult and tormenting moments.

This relationship with the Lord is not intended as a duty or an imposition. It is a bond that comes from within. It is *a relationship lived with the heart*; it is our friendship with God, granted to us by Jesus, a friendship that changes our life and fills us with passion, with joy. Thus, the gift of piety stirs in us, above all, gratitude and praise. This is, in fact, the reason for and *the most authentic meaning of our worship and our adoration*. When the Holy Spirit allows us to perceive the presence of the Lord and all his love for us, it warms the heart and moves us quite naturally to prayer and celebration. Piety, therefore, is synonymous with the genuine religious spirit, with filial trust in God, with that capacity to pray to him with the love and simplicity that belong to those who are humble of heart.

If the gift of piety makes us grow in relation to and in communion with God and leads us to live as his children, at the same time, it helps us *pass this love on to others as well and to recognize them as our brothers and sisters.* And then, yes, we will be moved by feelings of piety—not pietism!—in relation to those around us and to those we encounter every day. Why do I say "not

> *When the Holy Spirit allows us to perceive the presence of the Lord and all his love for us, it warms the heart and moves us quite naturally to prayer and celebration.*

pietism"? Because some think that to be pious is to close one's eyes, to pose like a picture and pretend to be a saint. In Piedmont we say to play the *mugna quacia* [literally: the pious or serene nun]. This is not the gift of piety. The gift of piety means to be truly capable of rejoicing with those who rejoice, of weeping with those who weep, of being close to those who are lonely or in anguish, of correcting those in error, of consoling the afflicted, of welcoming and helping those in need. The gift of piety is closely tied to gentleness. The gift of piety, which the Holy Spirit gives us, makes us gentle, makes us calm, patient, at peace with God, at the service of others with gentleness.

Dear friends, in the Letter to the Romans the apostle Paul states: "All who are guided by the Spirit of God are sons of God, for what you received was not the spirit of slavery to bring you back into fear; you received the spirit of adoption, enabling us to cry out, '*Abba*, Father!'" (Rom. 8:14–15, *NJB*). Let us ask the Lord for the gift of his Spirit to conquer our fear, our uncertainty, and our restless, impatient spirit, and to make of us joyful witnesses of God and of his love, by worshiping the Lord in truth and in service to our neighbor with gentleness and with a smile, which the Holy Spirit always gives us in joy. May the Holy Spirit grant to all of us this gift of piety.

23

Walking in the Fear of the Lord

General Audience, June 11, 2014

The gift of *fear of the Lord*, which we are speaking about today, concludes the series of the seven gifts of the Holy Spirit. By "fear of the Lord" we do not mean being afraid of God; we know well that God is Father, that he loves us and wants our salvation, and that he always forgives, always—thus, there is no reason to be scared of him!

Fear of the Lord, instead, is the gift of the Holy Spirit through whom we are reminded of how small we are before God, and of his love, and that our good lies in humble, respectful, and trusting self-abandonment into his hands. This is fear of the Lord: abandonment to the goodness of our Father who loves us so much.

When the Holy Spirit comes to dwell in our hearts, he infuses us with consolation and peace, and he leads us to the awareness of how small we are, with that attitude—strongly recommended by Jesus in the Gospel—of one who places his every care and expectation in God and feels enfolded and sustained by his warmth and protection, just as a child with his father! This is what the Holy Spirit does in our hearts: he makes us feel like children in the arms of our father. In this sense, then, we correctly comprehend how fear of the Lord in us takes on the form of docility, gratitude, and praise by filling our hearts with hope. Indeed, we frequently fail to grasp the plan of God, and we realize that we are not capable of assuring ourselves of happiness and eternal life. It is precisely in experiencing our own limitations and our poverty, however, that the Holy Spirit comforts us and lets us perceive that the only important thing is to allow ourselves to be led by Jesus into the Father's arms.

This is why we need this gift of the Holy Spirit so much. Fear of the Lord allows us to be aware that everything comes from grace and that our true strength lies solely in following the Lord Jesus and in allowing the Father to bestow

> *This is fear of the Lord: abandonment to the goodness of our Father who loves us so much.*

upon us his goodness and his mercy. [Fear of the Lord helps us] open the heart, so that the goodness and mercy of God may come to us. This is what the Holy Spirit does through the gift of fear of the Lord: he opens hearts. The heart opens so that forgiveness, mercy, goodness, and the caress of the Father may come to us, for as children we are infinitely loved.

When we are pervaded by fear of the Lord, then we are led to follow the Lord with humility, docility, and obedience. This, however, is not an attitude of resignation, passivity, or regret but one of the wonder and joy of being a child who knows he or she is served and loved by the Father. Fear of the Lord, therefore, does not make us Christians who are shy and submissive; [rather, it] stirs in us courage and strength! It is a gift that makes us Christians who are convinced, enthusiastic, who aren't submissive to the Lord out of fear but because we are moved and conquered by his love! To be conquered by the love of God! This is a beautiful thing. To allow ourselves to be conquered by this love of a father, who loves us so, loves us with all his heart.

Yet, we should take care, for the gift of God, the gift of fear of the Lord, is also an "alarm" against the obstinacy of sin. When a person lives in evil, when one blasphemes against God, when one exploits others or tyrannizes them or lives only for money, vanity, power, or pride, then the holy fear of God sends us a warning: be careful! With all this power, with all this money, with all your pride, with all your vanity, you will not be happy. No one can take it with [him or her] to the other side: not the money, power, vanity, or pride. Nothing! We can take only the love that God the Father gives us, God's embrace, accepted and received by us with love.

And we can take what we have done for others. Take care not to place your hope in money or pride, power, or vanity because they can promise you nothing good! I am thinking, for example, of people who have responsibility for others and allow themselves to become corrupt; do you think a corrupt person will be happy on the other side? No, all the fruit of corruption has corrupted the heart, and it will be difficult for the person to go to the Lord. I am thinking of those who live off human trafficking or slave labor; do you think these people who traffic persons, who exploit people through slave labor, have love for God in their hearts? No, they haven't fear of the Lord, and they are not happy. They are not. I am thinking of those who manufacture weapons for fomenting wars; just think about what kind of job this is. I am certain that if I were to ask, "How many of you manufacture weapons?" there would be no one, no one. These weapons manufacturers don't come to hear the Word of God! These people manufacture death; they are merchants of death, and they make death into a piece of merchandise. May fear of the Lord make them understand that one day all things will come to an end and they will have to give account to God.

PART FOUR

The Witness of the Walk

24

Inviting Others to Walk with Us

From the encyclical Lumen Fidei *("The Light of Faith"),*
June 29, 2013

Those who have opened their hearts to God's love, heard his voice, and received his light cannot keep this gift to themselves. Because faith is hearing and seeing, it is also handed on as word and light. Addressing the Corinthians, St. Paul used these very images. On the one hand, he says, "But just as we have the same spirit of faith that is in accordance with scripture—'I believed, and so I spoke'—we also believe, and so we speak" (2 Cor. 4:13). The word, once accepted, becomes a response, a confession of faith, which spreads to others and invites them to believe.

Paul also uses the image of light: "All of us, with unveiled faces, seeing the glory of the Lord as though reflected in a mirror, are being transformed into the same image" (2 Cor. 3:18). It is a light reflected from one face to another, even as Moses himself bore a reflection of God's glory after having spoken with him: "God . . . has shone in our hearts to give the light of the knowledge of the glory of God in the face of Christ" (2 Cor. 4:6). The light of Christ shines, as in a mirror, upon the face of Christians; as it spreads, it comes down to us, so that we, too, can share in that vision and reflect that light to others in the same way that, in the Easter liturgy, the light of the paschal candle lights countless other candles. Faith is passed on, we might say, by contact, from one person to another, just as one candle is lighted from another. Christians, in their poverty, plant a seed so rich that it becomes a great tree, capable of filling the world with its fruit.

The transmission of the faith not only brings light to men and women in every place; it travels through time, passing from one generation to another. Because faith is born of an encounter that takes place in history and lights up our journey through time, it must be passed on in every

Faith is passed on by contact, from one person to another, just as one candle is lighted from another.

age. It is through an unbroken chain of witnesses that we come to see the face of Jesus.

But how is this possible? How can we be certain, after all these centuries, that we have encountered the "real Jesus"? Were we merely isolated individuals, were our starting point simply our own individual ego seeking in itself the basis of absolutely sure knowledge, a certainty of this sort would be impossible. I cannot possibly verify for myself something that happened so long ago.

But this is not the only way we attain knowledge. [People] always live in relationship. We come from others, we belong to others, and our lives are enlarged by our encounter with others. Even our own knowledge and self-awareness are relational; they are linked to others who have gone before us: in the first place, our parents, who gave us our life and our name. Language itself, the words by which we make sense of our lives and the world around us, comes to us from others, preserved in the living memory of others. Self-knowledge is possible only when we share in a greater memory.

The same thing holds true for faith, which brings human understanding to its fullness. Faith's past, that act of Jesus' love that brought new life to the world, comes down to us through the memory of others—witnesses—and is kept alive in that one remembering subject that is the Church. The Church is a Mother who teaches us to speak the language of faith. St. John brings this out in his Gospel by closely uniting faith and memory and associating both with the working of the Holy Spirit, who, as Jesus says, "will remind you of all I have said to you" (John 14:26, *NJB*). The love which is the Holy Spirit and which dwells in the Church unites every age and makes us contemporaries of Jesus, thus guiding us along our pilgrimage of faith.

It is impossible to believe on our own. Faith is not simply an individual decision that takes place in the depths of the believer's heart, nor is it a completely private relationship between the "I" of the believer and the divine "Thou," between an autonomous subject and God. By its very nature, faith is open to the "We" of the Church; it always takes place within her communion.

We are reminded of this by the dialogical format of the Creed used in the baptismal liturgy. Our belief is expressed in response to an invitation, to a word that must be heard and that is not my own; it exists as part of a dialogue and cannot be merely a profession originating in an individual. We can respond in the singular—"I believe"—only because we are part of a greater fellowship, only because we also say, "We believe." This openness to the ecclesial "We" reflects the openness of God's own love, which is not only a relationship between the Father and the Son, between an "I" and a "Thou," but is also, in the Spirit, a "We," a communion of persons.

Here we see why those who believe are never alone and why faith tends to spread as it invites others to share in its joy. Those who receive faith discover that their horizons expand as new and enriching relationships come to life. Tertullian put this well when he described the catechumens who, "after the cleansing which gives new birth," are welcomed into the house of their mother and, as part of a new family, pray the Our Father together with their brothers and sisters.

25

To Make the Gospel Visible

Address to participants in the plenary of the Pontifical Council for Promoting the New Evangelization, October 14, 2013

Talking about passing on the faith, I would like to reflect on three points: the primacy of witness, the urgency of going out to meet others, and the need for a pastoral plan centered on the essential.

Often today there is an attitude of indifference toward the faith, an attitude that regards it as irrelevant for human life. The new evangelization means reawakening the life of faith in the minds and hearts of our contemporaries. Faith is a gift of God; however, it is important that we Christians demonstrate that we live faith in a concrete way—through love, harmony, joy, suffering—because this gives rise to questions similar to those raised at the beginning of the Church's journey: Why do they live that way? What urges them on? These questions lead straight to the heart of evangelization, to the witness of faith and charity. What we especially need in these times are credible witnesses who make the Gospel visible by their lives as well as by their words and who reawaken the attraction for Jesus Christ, for the beauty of God.

Many people have drifted away from the Church. It would be a mistake to place the blame on one side or the other; indeed, there is no need even to speak of blame. There were mistakes in the history of the Church and her men, [mistakes related to] certain ideologies and also individuals. As children of the Church we must continue on the journey of the Second Vatican

Council and divest ourselves of useless and hurtful things, of false worldly security that weighs down the Church and injures her true face. We need Christians who make God's mercy and tenderness for every creature visible to the men and women of our day.

We all know that the crisis of modern humanity is not superficial but profound. That is why the new evangelization, while it calls us to have the courage to swim against the tide and to be converted from idols to the true God, cannot but use a language of mercy expressed in gestures and attitudes even before words. The Church says as she stands amid humanity today: Come to Jesus, all you who labor and are heavy laden . . . and you will find rest for your souls (cf. Matt. 11:28–30). Come to Jesus. He alone has the words of eternal life.

Every baptized Christian is a "Christopher," namely, a Christ bearer, as the Church Fathers used to say. Whoever has encountered Christ, as did the Samaritan woman at the well, cannot keep this experience to themselves but feels the need to share it and to lead others to Jesus (cf. John 4). We all need to ask ourselves if those who encounter us perceive the warmth of faith in our lives, if they see in our faces the joy of having encountered Christ!

> *What we especially need in these times are credible witnesses who make the Gospel visible by their lives as well as by their words and who reawaken the attraction for Jesus Christ, for the beauty of God.*

Here we pass to the second aspect: encounter, *going out to meet others*. The new evangelization is a renewed movement toward those who have lost the faith and a sense of the deep meaning of life. This dynamism is part of Christ's great mission to bring life to the world, to bring the Father's love to humankind. The Son of God "went forth" from his divine condition and came to meet us. The Church abides within this movement; every Christian is called to go out to meet others, to dialogue with those who do not think as we do, with those who have another faith or who have no faith. To encounter all, because what we all share in common is that we were created in the image and likeness of God. We can go out to everyone without fear and without renouncing our membership in the Church.

No one is excluded from life's hope, from God's love. The Church is sent to reawaken this hope everywhere, especially where it has been suffocated by difficult and oftentimes inhuman living conditions; where hope cannot breathe, it suffocates. We need the fresh air of the Gospel, the breath of the Spirit of the Risen Christ, to rekindle it in people's hearts. The Church is the home where the doors are always open, not only because everyone finds a welcome and is able to breathe in love and hope, but also because we can go out bearing this love and this hope. The Holy Spirit urges us to go beyond our own narrow confines, and he guides us to the outskirts of humanity.

However, in the Church all of this cannot be left to chance or improvisation. It requires a shared commitment to a pastoral plan that brings us back to the essential and that is *solidly focused on the essential, that is, on Jesus Christ.* To get diverted by many secondary or superfluous things does not help; what helps is to focus on the fundamental reality, which is the encounter with Christ, with his mercy and with his love, and to love our brothers and sisters as he has loved us.

An encounter with Christ is also *adoration,* a little-used word: to adore Christ. We need a plan animated by the creativity and imagination of the Holy Spirit, who also urges us to take new paths with courage without becoming fossils! We might ask ourselves, what is the pastoral plan of our dioceses or parishes like? Does it make the essential visible, namely Jesus Christ? Do the various experiences and features that the Holy Spirit grants journey together in harmony? Or is our pastoral plan dissipated and fragmented, such that in the end everyone goes his or her own way?

In this context I would like to emphasize the importance of catechesis as a moment for evangelization. Pope Paul VI spoke of it some years ago in *Evangelii Nuntiandi* (cf. n. 44). Starting from there, the great catechetical movement has promoted renewal to overcome the split between the Gospel and culture and the illiteracy that exists today in matters of faith. I have recalled many times something that greatly impressed me in my ministry: meeting children who did not even know how to make the sign of the cross! In our cities! The role that catechists play is a truly valuable service for the new evangelization, and it is important that parents be the first catechists, the first educators of the faith in their own family by their witness and by their word.

26

Rich by Jesus' Poverty

Lenten message, December 26, 2014

As Lent draws near, I would like to offer some helpful thoughts on our path of conversion as individuals and as a community. These insights are inspired by the words of St. Paul: "For you know the grace of our Lord Jesus Christ, that though he was rich, yet for your sake he became poor, so that by his poverty you might become rich" (2 Cor. 8:9). The apostle was writing to the Christians of Corinth to encourage them to be generous in helping the faithful in Jerusalem who were in need. What do these words of St. Paul mean for us Christians today? What does this invitation to poverty, a life of evangelical poverty, mean for us today?

First of all, it shows us how God works. He does not reveal himself cloaked in worldly power and wealth but rather in weakness and poverty: "*though he was rich, yet for your sake he became poor.*" Christ, the eternal Son of God, one with the Father in power and glory, chose to be poor; he came among us and drew near to each of us; he set aside his glory and emptied himself so that he could be like us in all things (cf. Phil. 2:7; Heb. 4:15). God's becoming human is a great mystery! But the reason for all this is his love, a love that is grace, generosity, a desire to draw near, a love that does not hesitate to offer itself in sacrifice for the beloved.

Charity—love—shares in all things with the one we love. Love makes us similar, it creates equality, it breaks down walls and eliminates distances. God did this with us. Indeed, Jesus "worked with human hands, thought with a human mind, acted by human choice and loved with a human heart. Born of the Virgin Mary, he truly became one of us, like us in all things except sin" (*Gaudium et Spes*, 22).

By making himself poor, Jesus did not seek poverty for its own sake but, as St. Paul says, "*that by his poverty you might become rich.*" This is no mere play on words or a catchphrase. Rather, it sums up God's logic, the logic of love, the logic of the incarnation and the cross. God did not let our salvation drop down from heaven, like someone who gives alms from their abundance out of a sense of altruism and piety. Christ's love is different! When Jesus stepped into the waters of the Jordan and was baptized by John the Baptist, he did so not because he was in need of repentance, or conversion; he did it to be among people who need forgiveness, among us sinners, and to take upon himself the burden of our sins. In this way he chose to comfort us, to save us, to free us from our misery. It is striking that the apostle states that we were set free not by Christ's riches but *by his poverty*. Yet St. Paul is well aware of "the unsearchable riches of Christ" (Eph. 3:8), that he is "heir of all things" (Heb. 1:2).

So what is this poverty by which Christ frees us and enriches us? It is his way of loving us, his way of being our neighbor, just as the Good Samaritan was neighbor to the man left half dead by the side of the road (cf. Luke 10:25). What gives us true freedom, true salvation, and true happiness is the compassion, tenderness, and solidarity of his love. Christ's poverty, which enriches us, is his taking flesh and bearing our weaknesses and sins as an expression of God's infinite mercy to us.

> *Christ's poverty is the greatest treasure of all: his boundless confidence in God the Father, his constant trust, his desire always to do the Father's will and give glory to him.*

Christ's poverty is the greatest treasure of all: Jesus' wealth is that of his boundless confidence in God the Father, his constant trust, his desire always and only to do the Father's will and give glory to him. Jesus is rich in the same way as a child who feels loved and who loves his or her parents, without doubting their love and tenderness for an instant. Jesus' wealth lies in his being *the Son*; his unique relationship with the Father is the sovereign prerogative of this Messiah who is poor. When Jesus asks us to take up his "yoke, which is easy," he asks us to be enriched by his "poverty, which is rich" and his "richness, which is poor," to share his filial and fraternal Spirit, to become sons and daughters in the Son, brothers and sisters in the firstborn brother (cf. Rom. 8:29).

It has been said that the only real regret lies in not being a saint (L. Bloy); we could also say that there is only one real kind of poverty: not living as children of God and brothers and sisters of Christ.

We might think that this "way" of poverty was Jesus' way, whereas we who come after him can save the world with the right kind of *human* resources. This is not the case. In every time and place God continues to save humankind and the world *through the poverty of Christ*, who makes himself poor in the sacraments, in his word, and in his Church, which is a people of the poor. God's wealth passes not through our wealth but invariably and exclusively through our personal and communal poverty, enlivened by the Spirit of Christ.

In imitation of our Master, we Christians are called to confront the poverty of our brothers and sisters, to touch it, to make it our own, and to take practical steps to alleviate it. *Destitution* is not the same as *poverty*: destitution is poverty without faith, without support, without hope. There are three types of destitution: material, moral, and spiritual. *Material destitution* is what is normally called poverty, and it affects those living in conditions opposed to human dignity—those who lack basic rights and needs such as food, water, hygiene, work, and the opportunity to develop and grow culturally. In response to this destitution, the Church offers her help, her *diakonia*, in meeting these needs and binding these wounds that disfigure the face of humanity. In the poor and outcast we see Christ's face; by loving and helping the poor, we love and serve Christ. Our efforts are also directed to ending violations of human dignity, discrimination, and abuse in the world, for these are so often the cause of destitution. When power, luxury, and money become idols, they take priority over the need for a fair distribution of wealth. Our consciences thus need to be converted to justice, equality, simplicity, and sharing.

No less a concern is *moral destitution*, which consists in slavery to vice and sin. How much pain is caused in families because one of their members . . . is in thrall to alcohol, drugs, gambling, or pornography! How many people no longer see meaning in life or prospects for the future; how many have lost hope! And how many are plunged into this destitution by unjust social conditions, by unemployment, which takes away their dignity as breadwinners, and by lack of equal access to education and health care. In such cases, moral destitution can be considered impending suicide. This type of destitution, which also causes financial ruin, is invariably linked to the *spiritual destitution* we experience when we turn away from God and reject his love. If we think we don't need God, who reaches out to us through Christ, because we believe we can make do on our own, we are headed for a fall. God alone can truly save and free us.

The Gospel is the real antidote to spiritual destitution: wherever we go, we are called as Christians to proclaim the liberating news that forgiveness for sins committed is possible, that God is greater than our sinfulness, that he freely loves us at all times, and that we were made for communion and eternal life. The Lord asks us to be joyous heralds of this message of mercy and hope! It is thrilling to experience the joy of spreading this good news, sharing the treasure entrusted to us, consoling broken hearts, and offering hope to our brothers and sisters experiencing darkness. It means following and imitating Jesus, who sought out the poor and sinners as a shepherd lovingly seeks his lost sheep. In union with Jesus, we can courageously open up new paths of evangelization and human promotion.

[. . .] [M]ay [the] Lenten season find the whole Church ready to bear witness to all those who live in material, moral, and spiritual destitution, to the Gospel message of the merciful love of God our Father, who is ready to embrace everyone in Christ. We can do this to the extent that we imitate Christ, who became poor and enriched us by his poverty. Lent is a fitting time for self-denial; we would do well to ask ourselves what we can give up in order to help and enrich others by our own poverty. Let us not forget that real poverty hurts: no self-denial is real without this dimension of penance. I distrust a charity that costs nothing and does not hurt.

May the Holy Spirit, through whom we are "as poor, yet making many rich; as having nothing, and yet possessing everything" (2 Cor. 6:10), sustain us in our resolutions and increase our concern and responsibility for human destitution so that we can become merciful and act with mercy. [. . .]

27

The Beatitudes:
Revolutionary Path to Joy

Message for the Twenty-Ninth World Youth Day, January 21, 2014

It is always a joyful experience for us to read and reflect on the Beatitudes! Jesus proclaimed them in his first great sermon, preached on the shore of the Sea of Galilee. There was a very large crowd, so Jesus went up on the mountain to teach his disciples. That is why it is known as "the Sermon on the Mount." In the Bible, the mountain is regarded as a place where God reveals himself. Jesus, by preaching on the mount, reveals himself to be a divine teacher, a new Moses. What does he tell us? He shows us the way to life, the way that he himself has taken. Jesus himself *is* the way, and he proposes this way as *the path to true happiness*. Throughout his life, from his birth in the stable in Bethlehem until his death on the cross and his resurrection, Jesus embodied the Beatitudes. All the promises of God's kingdom were fulfilled in him.

In proclaiming the Beatitudes, Jesus asks us to follow him and to travel with him along the path of love, the path that alone leads to eternal life. It is not an easy journey, yet the Lord promises us his grace, and he never abandons us. We face so many challenges in life: poverty, distress, humiliation, the struggle for justice, persecutions, the difficulty of daily conversion, the effort to remain faithful to our call to holiness, and many others. But if we open the door to Jesus and allow him to be part of our lives, if we share our joys and sorrows with him, then we will experience the peace and joy that only God, who is infinite love, can give.

The Beatitudes of Jesus are new and revolutionary. They present a model of happiness contrary to what is usually communicated by the media and by the prevailing wisdom. A worldly way of thinking finds it scandalous that God became one of us and died on a cross! According to the logic of this world, those whom Jesus proclaimed blessed are regarded as useless "losers." What is glorified is success at any cost, affluence, the arrogance of power, and self-affirmation at the expense of others.

Jesus challenges us [. . .] to take seriously his approach to life and to decide which path is right for us and leads to true joy. This is the great challenge of faith. Jesus was not afraid to ask his disciples if they truly wanted to follow him or if they preferred to take another path (cf. John 6:67). Simon Peter had the courage to reply: "Lord, to whom shall we go? You have the words of eternal life" (John 6:68). If you, too, are able to say yes to Jesus, your lives will become both meaningful and fruitful.

In an age when we are constantly being enticed by vain and empty illusions of happiness, we risk settling for less and "thinking small" when it comes to the meaning of life.

What does it mean to be "blessed" (*makárioi* in Greek)? To be blessed means to be happy. Tell me: do you really want to be happy? In an age when we are constantly being enticed by vain and empty illusions of happiness, we risk settling for less and "thinking small" when it comes to the meaning of life. Think big instead! Open your hearts! As Blessed Pier Giorgio Frassati once said, "To live without faith, to have no heritage to uphold, to fail to struggle constantly to defend the truth: this is not living. It is scraping by. We should never just scrape by, but really live" (Letter to I. Bonini, 27 February 1925). In his homily on the day of Pier Giorgio Frassati's beatification (20 May 1990), John Paul II called him "a man of the Beatitudes" (AAS 82 [1990], 1518).

If you are really open to the deepest aspirations of your hearts, you will realize that you possess an unquenchable thirst for happiness, and this will allow you to expose and reject the "low-cost" offers and approaches all around you. When we look only for success, pleasure, and possessions and we turn these into idols, we may well have moments of exhilaration, an illusory sense of satisfaction, but ultimately we become enslaved, never satisfied, always looking for more. It is a tragic thing to see a young person who "has everything" but is weary and weak.

St. John, writing to young people, told them: "You are strong, and the word of God abides in you, and you have overcome the evil one" (1 John 2:14). Young people who choose Christ are strong: they are fed by his word, and they do not need to "stuff themselves" with other things! Have the courage to swim against the tide. Have the courage to be truly happy! Say no to an ephemeral, superficial, and throwaway culture, a culture that assumes that you are incapable of taking on responsibility and facing the great challenges of life!

28

"Blessed are the poor in spirit . . ."

Message for the Twenty-Ninth World Youth Day, January 21, 2014

The first Beatitude says that *the poor in spirit* are blessed, for theirs is the kingdom of heaven. At a time when so many people are suffering as a result of the financial crisis, it might seem strange to link poverty and happiness. How can we consider poverty a blessing?

First of all, let us try to understand what it means to be "poor in spirit." When the Son of God became human, he chose the path of poverty and self-emptying. As St. Paul said in his letter to the Philippians: "Let the same mind be in you that was in Christ Jesus, who, though he was in the form of God, did not count equality with God a thing to be grasped, but emptied himself, taking the form of a servant, being born in human likeness" (2:5–7). Jesus is God who strips himself of his glory. Here we see God's choice to be poor: he was rich and yet he became poor in order to enrich us through his poverty (cf. 2 Cor. 8:9). This is the mystery we contemplate when we see the Son of God lying in a manger, and later on the cross, where his self-emptying reaches its culmination.

The Greek adjective *ptochós* (poor) does not have a purely material meaning. It means "a beggar," and it should be seen as linked to the Jewish notion of the *anawim*, "God's poor." It suggests lowliness, a sense of one's limitations and existential poverty. The *anawim* trust in the Lord, and they know that they can count on him.

As St. Thérèse of the Child Jesus clearly saw, by his incarnation Jesus came among us as a poor beggar, asking for our love. *The Catechism of the Catholic Church* tells us that "man is a beggar before God" (n. 2559) and that prayer is the encounter of God's thirst and our own thirst (n. 2560).

St. Francis of Assisi understood perfectly the secret of the Beatitude of the poor in spirit. Indeed, when Jesus spoke to him through the leper and from the crucifix, Francis recognized both God's grandeur and his own lowliness. In his prayer, the Poor Man of Assisi would spend hours asking the Lord, "Who are you?" "Who am I?" He renounced an affluent and carefree life in order to marry "Lady Poverty" to imitate Jesus and to follow the Gospel to the letter. Francis lived in *imitation of Christ in his poverty and in love for the poor*—for him the two were inextricably linked, like two sides of one coin.

You might ask me, then, What can we do, specifically, to make poverty in spirit a way of life, a real part of our own lives? I will reply by saying three things.

First of all, try to be *free with regard to material things*. The Lord calls us to a Gospel lifestyle marked by sobriety, by a refusal to yield to the culture of consumerism. This means being concerned with the essentials and learning to do without all those unneeded extras that hem us in. Let us learn to be detached from possessiveness and from the idolatry of money and lavish spending. Let us put Jesus first. He can free us from the kinds of idol worship that enslave us. Put your trust in God, dear young friends! He knows and loves us, and he never forgets us. Just as he provides for the lilies of the field (cf. Matt. 6:28), so he will make sure that we lack nothing. If we are to come through the financial crisis, we must be also ready to change our lifestyle and avoid so much wastefulness. Just as we need the courage to be happy, we also need the courage to live simply.

> *Let us learn to be detached from possessiveness and from the idolatry of money and lavish spending. Let us put Jesus first. He can free us from the kinds of idol worship that enslave us.*

Second, if we are to live by this Beatitude, all of us need to experience a *conversion in the way we see the poor*. We have to care for them and be sensitive to their spiritual and material needs. To [. . .] young people I especially entrust the task of restoring solidarity to the heart of human culture. Faced with old and new forms of poverty—unemployment, migration, and addictions of various kinds—we have the duty to be alert and thoughtful, avoiding the temptation to remain indifferent. We have to remember all those who feel unloved, who have no hope for the future, and who have given up on life out of discouragement, disappointment, or fear. We have to learn to be on the side of the poor and not just indulge in rhetoric about the poor! Let us go out to meet them, look into their eyes, and listen to them. The poor provide us with a concrete opportunity to encounter Christ himself and to touch his suffering flesh.

However—and this is my third point—the poor are not just people to whom we can give something. *They have much to offer us and to teach us.* How much we have to learn from the wisdom of the poor! Think about it: several hundred years ago a saint, Benedict Joseph Labré, who lived on the streets of Rome from the alms he received, became a spiritual guide to all sorts of people, including nobles and prelates. In a very real way, the poor are our teachers. They show us that people's value is not measured by their possessions or how much money they have in the bank. A poor person, a person lacking material possessions, always maintains his or her dignity. The poor can teach us much about humility and trust in God. In the parable of the Pharisee and the tax collector (cf. Luke 18:9–14), Jesus holds the tax collector up as a model because of his humility and his acknowledgment that he is a sinner. The widow who gave her last two coins to the temple treasury is an example of the generosity of all those who have next to nothing and yet give away everything they have (Luke 21:1–4).

29

" . . . for theirs is the kingdom of heaven."

Message for the Twenty-Ninth World Youth Day, January 21, 2014

The central theme of the Gospel is the kingdom of God. Jesus is the kingdom of God *in person*; he is Immanuel, God with us. And it is in the human heart that the kingdom, God's sovereignty, takes root and grows. The kingdom is at once both gift and promise. It has already been given to us in Jesus, but it has yet to be realized in its fullness. That is why we pray to the Father each day, "Thy kingdom come."

There is a close connection between poverty and evangelization, between the theme of the last World Youth Day—"Go therefore, and make disciples of all nations" (Matt. 28:19)—and the theme for this year [2014], "Blessed are the poor in spirit, for theirs is the kingdom of heaven" (Matt. 5:3). The Lord wants a poor Church that evangelizes the poor. When Jesus sent the Twelve out on mission, he said to them, "Take no gold, nor silver, nor copper in your belts, no bag for your journey, nor two tunics, nor sandals, nor a staff; for the laborers deserve their food" (Matt. 10:9–10). Evangelical poverty is a basic condition for spreading the kingdom of God. The most beautiful and spontaneous expressions of joy I have seen during my life were by poor people who had little to hold on to. Evangelization in our time will take place only as the result of contagious joy.

We have seen, then, that the Beatitude of the poor in spirit shapes our relationship with God, with material goods, and with the poor. With the example and words of Jesus before us, we realize how much we need to be converted so that the logic of *being more* will prevail over that

> The kingdom is both gift and promise. It has already been given to us in Jesus, but it has yet to be realized in its fullness.

of *having more*! The saints can best help us understand the profound meaning of the Beatitudes. So the canonization of John Paul II, to be celebrated on the Second Sunday of Easter, will be an event marked by immense joy. He will be the great patron of the World Youth Days, which he inaugurated and always supported. In the communion of saints he will continue to be a father and friend to all of you.

[. . .] April [2014] marks the thirtieth anniversary of the entrustment of the Jubilee Cross of the Redemption to the young. That symbolic act by John Paul II was the beginning of the great youth pilgrimage, which has since crossed the five continents. The Pope's words on that Easter Sunday in 1984 remain memorable: "My dear young people, at the conclusion of the Holy Year, I entrust to you the sign of this Jubilee Year: the cross of Christ! Carry it throughout the world as a symbol of the love of the Lord Jesus for humanity, and proclaim to everyone that it is only in Christ, who died and rose from the dead, that salvation and redemption are to be found." [. . .]

[T]he Magnificat, the Canticle of Mary, poor in spirit, is also the song of everyone who lives by the Beatitudes. The joy of the Gospel arises from a heart that, in its poverty, rejoices and marvels at the works of God, like the heart of Our Lady, whom all generations call "blessed" (cf. Luke 1:48). May Mary, Mother of the poor and Star of the new evangelization, help us live the Gospel, to embody the Beatitudes in our lives, and to have the courage always to be happy.

30

The Culture of Encounter

Message for the Forty-Eighth World Communications Day,
January 24, 2014

Today we are living in a world that is growing ever "smaller" and where, as a result, it would seem to be easier for all of us to be neighbors. Developments in travel and communications technology are bringing us closer together and making us more connected, even as globalization makes us increasingly interdependent. Nonetheless, divisions, which are sometimes quite deep, continue to exist within our human family. On the global level we see a scandalous gap between the opulence of the wealthy and the utter destitution of the poor. Often we need only walk the streets of a city to see the contrast between people living on the street and the brilliant lights of the store windows. We have become so accustomed to these things that they no longer unsettle us. Our world suffers from many forms of exclusion, marginalization, and poverty, to say nothing of conflicts born of a combination of economic, political, ideological, and, sadly, even religious motives.

In a world such as this one, media can help us feel closer to one another, creating a sense of the unity of the human family, which can in turn inspire solidarity and serious efforts to ensure a more dignified life for all. Good communication helps us grow closer, to know one another better and, ultimately, to grow in unity. The walls that divide us can be broken down only if we are prepared to listen and learn from one another. We need to resolve our differences through forms of dialogue that help us grow in understanding and mutual respect. A culture of encounter demands that we be ready not only to give but also to receive. Media can help us greatly in this, especially nowadays, when the networks of human communication have made unprecedented advances. The Internet, in particular, offers immense possibilities for encounter and solidarity. This is something truly good, a gift from God.

This is not to say that certain problems do not exist. The speed with which information is communicated exceeds our capacity for reflection and judgment, and this does not make for more balanced and proper forms of self-expression. The variety of opinions being aired can be seen as helpful, but it also enables people to barricade themselves behind sources of information that only confirm their own wishes and ideas or their political and economic interests. The world of communications can help us either to expand our knowledge or to lose our bearings. The desire for digital connectivity can have the effect of isolating us from our neighbors, from those closest to us. We should not overlook the fact that those who, for whatever reason, lack access to social media run the risk of being left behind.

While these drawbacks are real, they do not justify rejecting social media; rather, they remind us that communication is ultimately a human rather than a technological achievement. What is it, then, that helps us, in the digital environment, to grow in humanity and mutual understanding? We need, for example, to recover a certain sense of deliberateness and calm. This calls for time and the ability to be silent and to listen. We need also to be patient if

In a world such as this one, media can help us feel closer to one another, creating a sense of the unity of the human family, which can in turn inspire solidarity and serious efforts to ensure a more dignified life for all.

we want to understand those who are different from us. People express themselves fully only when they are not merely tolerated but know that they are truly accepted. If we are genuinely attentive in listening to others, we will learn to look at the world with different eyes and come to appreciate the richness of human experience as manifested in different cultures and traditions. We will also learn to appreciate more fully the important values inspired by

Christianity, such as the vision of the human person, the nature of marriage and the family, the proper distinction between the religious and political spheres, the principles of solidarity and subsidiarity, and many others.

How, then, can communication be at the service of an authentic culture of encounter? What does it mean for us, as disciples of the Lord, to encounter others in the light of the Gospel? In spite of our own limitations and sinfulness, how do we draw truly close to one another? These questions are summed up in what a scribe—a communicator—once asked Jesus: "And who is my neighbor?" (Luke 10:29). This question can help us see communication in terms of neighborliness. We might paraphrase the question in this way: how can we be "neighborly" in our use of the communications media and in the new environment created by digital technology? I find an answer in the parable of the Good Samaritan, which is also a parable about communication. Those who communicate, in effect, become neighbors. The Good Samaritan not only draws nearer to the man he finds half dead on the side of the road; he also takes responsibility for him. Jesus shifts our understanding: it is not just about seeing the other as someone like myself but also about the ability to make myself like the other. Communication is really about realizing that we are all human beings, children of God. I like seeing this power of communication as neighborliness.

Whenever communication is primarily aimed at promoting consumption or manipulating others, we are dealing with a form of violent aggression like that suffered by the man in the parable who was beaten by robbers and left abandoned on the road. The Levite and the priest do not regard him as a neighbor but as a stranger to be kept at a distance. In those days, it was rules of ritual purity that conditioned their response. Nowadays there is a danger that certain media so condition our responses that we fail to see our real neighbor.

It is not enough to be passersby on the digital highways, simply "connected"; connections need to grow into true encounters. We cannot live apart, closed in on ourselves. We need to love and to be loved. We need tenderness. Media strategies do not ensure beauty, goodness, and truth in communication. The world of media also has to be concerned with humanity; it, too, is called to show tenderness. The digital world can be an environment rich in humanity, a network not of wires but of people. The impartiality of media is merely an appearance; only those who go out of themselves in their communication can become a true point of reference for others. Personal engagement is the basis of the trustworthiness of a communicator. Christian witness, thanks to the Internet, can thereby reach the peripheries of human existence.

As I have frequently observed, if a choice has to be made between a bruised Church that goes out to the streets and a Church suffering from self-absorption, I certainly prefer the first. Those "streets" are the world where people live and where they can be reached, both effectively and affectively. The digital highway is one of them, a street teeming with people who are often hurting, men and women looking for salvation or hope. By means of the Internet, the Christian message can reach "to the ends of the earth" (Acts 1:8). Keeping the doors of our churches open also means keeping them open in the digital environment so that people, whatever their situation in life, can enter and so that the Gospel can go out to reach everyone. We are called to show that the Church is the home of all. Are we capable of communicating the image of such a Church? Communication is a means of expressing the missionary vocation of the entire Church; today the social networks are one way to experience this call to discover the beauty of faith, the beauty of encountering Christ. In the area of communications, too, we need a Church capable of bringing warmth and of stirring hearts.

Effective Christian witness is not about bombarding people with religious messages but about our willingness to be available to others "by patiently and respectfully engaging their questions and their doubts as they advance in their search for the truth and the meaning of human existence" (Benedict XVI, Message for the Forty-Seventh World Communications Day, 2013). We need but recall the story of the disciples on the way to Emmaus. We have to be able to dialogue with the men and women of today, to understand their expectations, doubts, and hopes, and to bring them the Gospel: Jesus Christ himself, God incarnate, who died and rose to free us from sin and death. We are challenged to be people of depth, attentive to what is happening around us, and spiritually alert. To dialogue means to believe that the "other" has something worthwhile to say and to entertain his or her point of view and perspective. Engaging in dialogue does not mean renouncing our own ideas and traditions but the claim that they alone are valid or absolute.

May the image of the Good Samaritan, who tended to the wounds of the injured man by pouring oil and wine over them, be our inspiration. Let our communication be a balm that relieves pain and a fine wine that gladdens hearts. May the light we bring to others not be the result of cosmetics or special effects, but rather of our being loving and merciful neighbors to those wounded and left on the side of the road. Let us boldly become citizens of the digital world. The Church needs to be concerned for, and present in, the world of communication, in order to dialogue with people today and to help them encounter Christ. She needs to be a Church at the side of others, capable of accompanying everyone along the way. The revolution taking place in communications media and in information technologies represents a great and thrilling challenge; may we respond to that challenge with fresh energy and imagination as we seek to share with others the beauty of God.

PART FIVE

To Accompany on the Walk

31

The Time of Mercy

Address to the parish priests of the Diocese of Rome, March 6, 2014

"Jesus went through all the towns and villages, teaching in their synagogues, proclaiming the good news of the kingdom and healing every disease and sickness. When he saw the crowds, he had compassion on them, because they were harassed and helpless, like sheep without a shepherd" (Matt. 9:35–36). The passage from the Gospel of Matthew makes us turn our gaze to Jesus as he goes about the cities and villages. And this is curious. Where was Jesus most often, where could he most easily be found? On the road. He might have seemed to be homeless because he was always on the road. Jesus' life was on the road. He especially invites us to grasp the depths of his heart, what he feels for the crowds, for the people he encounters: that interior attitude of "compassion"; seeing the crowds, he felt compassion for them. For he saw the people were "harassed and helpless, like sheep without a shepherd." We have heard these words so many times that perhaps they do not strike us powerfully. But they are powerful! A little like the many people you meet today on the streets of your own neighborhoods. . . . Then the horizon broadens, and we see that these towns and villages are not only Rome and Italy; they are the world . . . and those helpless crowds are the peoples of many nations who are suffering through even more difficult situations. . . .

Thus we understand that we are not here to take part in a pleasant retreat at the beginning of Lent, but rather to hear the voice of the Spirit speaking to the whole Church of our time, which is the time of mercy. I am sure of this. It is not only Lent; we are living in a time of mercy and have been for thirty years or more, up to today.

This was an intuition of St. John Paul II. He "sensed" that this was the time of mercy. We think of the beatification and canonization of Sister Faustina Kowalska; then he introduced the Feast of Divine Mercy. Little by little he advanced and went forward on this.

In his homily for the canonization, which took place in 2000, John Paul II emphasized that the message of Jesus Christ to Sister Faustina is located, in time, between the two World Wars and is intimately tied to the history of the twentieth century. And looking to the future, he said, "What will the years ahead bring us? What will man's future on earth be like? We are not given to know. However, it is certain that in addition to new progress there will unfortunately be no lack of painful experiences. But the light of divine mercy, which the Lord in a way wished to return to the world through Sister Faustina's charism, will illumine the way for the men and women of the third millennium" (Homily, Sunday, April 30, 2000). It is clear. Here it is explicit, in 2000, but it was something that had been maturing in his heart for some time. Through his prayer, he had this intuition.

Today we forget everything far too quickly, even the Magisterium of the Church! Part of this is unavoidable, but we cannot forget the great content, the great intuitions and gifts that have been left to the People of God. And divine mercy is one of these. It is a gift he gave to us but which comes from above. It is up to us, as ministers of the Church, to keep this message alive, above all through preaching and in our actions, in signs and in pastoral choices, such as the decision to restore priority to the sacrament of reconciliation and to the works of mercy. Reconciliation—making peace through the sacrament, also with words, and with works of mercy. [. . .]

Let us ask ourselves what mercy means for a priest. [. . .] Priests are moved to compassion before the sheep, like Jesus, when he saw the people harassed and helpless, like sheep without a shepherd. Jesus has the "bowels" of God; Isaiah speaks about it very much; he is full of tenderness for the people, especially for those who are excluded, that is, for sinners, for the sick whom no one takes care of. . . . Thus, in the image of the Good Shepherd, the priest is a man of mercy and compassion, close to his people and a servant to all.

This is a pastoral criterion I would like to emphasize strongly: closeness. Closeness and service, but closeness, nearness! . . . Whoever is wounded in life, in whatever way, can find in him attention and a sympathetic ear. . . . The priest reveals a heart especially in administering the sacrament of reconciliation; he reveals it by his whole attitude, by the manner in which he welcomes, listens, counsels, and absolves. . . . But this comes from how he experiences the sacrament firsthand, from how he allows himself to be embraced by God the Father in confession and remains in this embrace. . . . If one experiences this in one's own regard, in his own heart, he can also give it to others in his ministry.

And I leave you with the question: how do I confess? Do I allow myself to be embraced? A great priest from Buenos Aires comes to mind; he is younger than me, around the age of seventy-two . . . Once he came to see me. He is a great confessor: there are always people waiting in line for him there. . . . The majority of priests confess to him . . . And once he came to see me: "But Father . . . Tell me . . . I have a small scruple, because I know that I forgive too much!" "Pray . . . if you forgive too much. . . ." And we spoke about mercy. At a certain point he said to me: "You know, when I feel this scruple keenly, I go to the chapel, before the tabernacle, and I say to him, 'Excuse me, but it's your fault, because it is you who have given me the bad example!' And I go away at peace. . . ." It is a beautiful prayer of mercy! If one experiences this in his own regard in confession, in his own heart, he is able to give it to others.

The priest is called to learn this, to have a heart that is moved. Priests who are—allow me to say the word—"aseptic," those "from the laboratory," all clean and tidy, do not help the Church. Today we can think of the Church as a field hospital. Excuse me, but I repeat it, because this is how I see it, how I feel it is a field hospital. Wounds need to be treated, so many wounds! So many wounds! There are so many people who are wounded by material problems, by scandals, also in the Church. . . . People wounded by the world's illusions. . . . We priests must be there, close to these people. Mercy first means treating the wounds. When someone is wounded, he needs this immediately, not tests such as the level of cholesterol and one's glycemic index . . . But there's a wound; treat the wound, and then we can look at the results of the tests. Then specialized treatments can be done, but first we need to treat the open wounds. I think this is what is most important at this time.

And there are also hidden wounds, because there are people who distance themselves in order to avoid showing their wounds. . . . The custom comes to mind, in the Mosaic law, of the lepers in Jesus' time who were always kept at a distance in order not to spread the contagion. . . . There are people who distance themselves through shame, so as not to let their wounds be seen. . . . And perhaps they distance themselves with some bitterness against the Church, but deep down inside there is a wound. . . . They want a caress! [. . .] I ask [priests]—do you know the wounds of your parishioners? Do you perceive them? Are you close to them? It's the only question. . . .

Let us return to the sacrament of reconciliation. It often happens that we priests hear our faithful telling us they have encountered a very "strict" priest in the confessional, or a very "generous" one—that is, a *rigorist* or a *laxist*. And this is not good. It is normal that there be differences in the style of confessors, but these differences cannot disregard the essential, that is, sound moral doctrine and mercy. Neither the laxist nor the rigorist bears witness to Jesus Christ, for neither the one nor the other takes care of the people he encounters. The rigorist washes his hands of them: in fact, he nails them to the law, understood in a cold and rigid way. And the laxist also washes his hands of them; he is only apparently merciful, but in reality he does not take seriously the problems of that conscience, by minimizing the sin.

True mercy *takes the person into one's care*, listens to him or her attentively, approaches the situation with respect and truth, and accompanies him or her on the journey of reconciliation. And this is demanding, yes, certainly. The truly merciful priest behaves like the Good Samaritan . . . but why does he do it? Because his heart is capable of having compassion; it is the heart of Christ!

We are well aware that *neither laxity nor rigorism fosters holiness*. Perhaps some rigorists seem holy, holy. . . . But think of Pelagius and then let's talk. . . . Neither laxity nor rigorism sanctify the priest, and they do not sanctify the faithful!

> Do you struggle with the Lord for your people, as Abraham struggled? Do you argue with the Lord as Moses did?

However, mercy accompanies the journey of holiness; it accompanies it and makes it grow. . . . Too much work for a parish priest? It is true, too much work! And how do we accompany and foster the journey of holiness? Through pastoral suffering, which is a form of mercy. What does pastoral suffering mean? It means suffering for and with the person. And this is not easy! To suffer like a father and mother suffer for their children; I venture to say, also with anxious concern. . . .

To explain, I'll put to you some questions that help me when a priest comes to me. They also help me when I am alone before the Lord! Tell me, do you weep? Or have we lost our tears? I remember that in the old Missals, those of another age, there is a most beautiful prayer to ask for the gift of tears. The prayer began like this: "Lord, who commanded Moses to strike the rock so that water might gush forth, strike the stone of my heart so that tears . . ."; the prayer went more or less like this. It was very beautiful. But how many of us weep before the suffering of a child, before the breakup of a family, before so many people who do not find the path? [. . .]

Do you weep for your people? Tell me, do you offer intercessory prayer before the tabernacle?

Do you struggle with the Lord for your people, as Abraham struggled? "Suppose they were fewer? Suppose there were twenty-five? And suppose they were twenty? . . ." (cf. Gen. 18:22–33). This courageous prayer of intercession. . . . We speak of *parrhesía*, of apostolic courage, and we think of pastoral plans; this is good, but the same *parrhesía* is also needed in prayer. Do you struggle with the Lord? Do you argue with the Lord as Moses did? When the Lord was annoyed, tired of his people, he said to him, "Don't worry. . . . I will destroy everything, and I will make you the head of another people." "No. No. If you destroy the people, destroy me, too." But these were real men! Do we have enough guts to struggle with God for our people?

Another question I ask: in the evening, how do you conclude your day? With the Lord or in front of the television? How is your relationship with those who help you to be more merciful? That is, how is your relationship with the children, with the elderly, with the sick? Do you know how to reassure them, or are you embarrassed to caress an elderly person?

Do not be ashamed of the flesh of your brother (cf. *Reflexiones en esperanza*, ch. 1). In the end, we will be judged on our ability to draw close to "all flesh"—this is Isaiah. Do not be ashamed of the flesh of your brother. "Making ourselves close": closeness, nearness, being close to the flesh of one's brother. The priest and the Levite who had passed by before the Good Samaritan did not know how to draw close to the person who had been beaten by bandits. Their hearts were closed. Perhaps the priest had looked at his watch and said, "I have to go to Mass; I cannot be late for Mass," and he left. Excuses! How often we justify ourselves to get around the problem, the person. The other, the Levite, or the doctor of the law, the lawyer, said, "No, I cannot because if I do this tomorrow, I will have to go and testify. I will lose time. . . ." Excuses! . . . Their hearts were closed. But a closed heart always justifies itself for what it has not done. Instead, the Samaritan opens his heart; he allows his heart to be moved, and this interior movement translates into practical action, in a concrete and effective intervention to help the person.

At the end of time, only those who have not been ashamed of the flesh of their brother who is injured and excluded will be permitted to contemplate the glorified flesh of Christ.

I admit, sometimes it does me good to read the list on which I will be judged; it benefits me: it is contained in Matthew 25. [. . .]

In Buenos Aires—I am speaking of another priest—there was a well-known confessor: he was a Sacramentine. Almost all the priests confessed to him. On one of the two occasions he came, John Paul II had requested a confessor at the Nunciature, and he went. He was old, very old. . . . He had served as Provincial in his order, as a professor . . . but always as a confessor, always. And a long line was always awaiting him in the Church of the Most Blessed Sacrament.

At the time, I was Vicar General and was living in the Curia, and every morning, early, I would go down to the fax to see if anything was there. And on Easter morning I read a fax from the community superior: "Yesterday, a half-hour before the Easter Vigil, Fr. Aristi died at the age of 94—or 96? The funeral will be on such and such a day. . . ." And on Easter morning I was to go to lunch with the priests at the retirement home—I usually did on Easter—and then I said to myself, *After lunch I will go to the church.* It was a large church, very large, with a beautiful crypt. I went down into the crypt, and the coffin was there; only two elderly women were praying there, but not a single flower. I thought, *But this man, who forgave the sins of all the clergy of Buenos Aires, including mine, not even a flower.* . . . I went up and went to a florist—because in Buenos Aires there are flower shops at the crossroads, on the streets, where there are people—and I bought flowers, roses. . . . And I returned and began to decorate the coffin with flowers. . . .

And I looked at the rosary in his hands. . . . And immediately it came to mind—the thief that we all have inside of us, don't we? And while I was arranging the flowers, I took the cross off the rosary, and with a little effort I detached it. At that moment I looked at him and said, "Give me half of your mercy." I felt something powerful that gave me the courage to do this and to say this prayer! And then I put the cross here, in my pocket. But the Pope's shirts don't have pockets, but I always carry it here in a little cloth bag, and that cross has been with me from that moment until today. And when an uncharitable thought against someone comes to mind, my hand always touches it here, always. And I feel the grace! I feel its benefit. What good the example of a merciful priest does, of a priest who draws close to wounds. . . .

If you think about it, surely you have known many, many of them, because Italian priests are good! They are good. I believe that if Italy is still so strong, it is not because of us who are bishops; rather, it is because of the parish priests, the priests! It is true, this is true! It is not a little incense to comfort you; I truly believe it to be so.

Mercy. Think of the many priests who are in heaven, and ask of them this grace! May they grant you the mercy they had with their faithful. This does good.

32

Feeding the People of God

Address to the community of the Pontifical Leonine College
in Anagni, April 14, 2014

[. . .] The "Leonine," as a regional seminary, serves several of the dioceses in Lazio. In line with its formative tradition it is called, in the Church today, to offer candidates to the priesthood a vital experience that transforms their vocational aspiration into a fruitful apostolic reality. Every seminary, yours too, aims to prepare future ordained ministers in a climate of prayer, study, and fraternity. It is this evangelical atmosphere, this life full of the Holy Spirit and of humanity, that allows those who immerse themselves therein to assimilate day by day the mind of Jesus Christ, his love for the Father and for the Church, his unreserved dedication to the People of God. Prayer, study, fraternity, and also apostolic life: these are the four pillars of formation, which interact. A strong spiritual life, a deep intellectual life, community life, and apostolic life—with no order of importance. All four are important. If one of them is missing, formation is not comprehensive. And these four interact. They are four pillars, four elements on which a seminary must base its life.

[. . .] [S]eminarians are not preparing for a career to become officials in a company or office. We have many, many priests who have gone only halfway. It is a source of sorrow that they have not attained fullness: there is something of an official in them, a bureaucratic element that does not benefit the Church. I urge you, be careful not to fall into this! You are becoming shepherds in the image of Jesus the Good Shepherd, in order to be like him and to act *in his person* amid his flock, to feed his sheep.

In view of this vocation, we might respond as Mary did to the angel: "How can this be?" (Luke 1:34). Becoming good shepherds in the image of Jesus is something too great, and we are too little. . . . It is true! Over the past days, I have been thinking of the Holy Thursday Chrism Mass, and I have felt this, that our little-

Always go to confession! And thus shall you become generous and merciful ministers because you will feel God's mercy upon you.

ness is made strong through this great gift that we receive: we are among the least of men. It is true, it is too great; however, it is not our work! It is the work of the Holy Spirit, with our cooperation. It is a matter of humbly offering oneself as clay to be molded so that the potter, who is God, may work it with water and fire, with the Word and the Spirit. It is a matter of entering into what St. Paul says: "It is no longer I who live, but Christ who lives in me" (Gal. 2:20). Only thus can one be a deacon or priest in the Church, only thus can we feed God's people and guide them, not along our ways but on the way of Jesus—indeed, on the *Way* that is Jesus.

It is true that there is not always a complete rectitude of intention right from the start [of a priest's formation]. However, I would daresay, it is difficult that this be so. All of us have always had these little things that were not consistent with an upright intention, but this resolves itself in time, through ongoing daily conversion. Let us think about the apostles! Think of James and John; one wanted to become the prime minister and the other the minister of the economy, because it was more important. The apostles still did not have this uprightness, their minds were elsewhere, and the Lord with great patience corrected their intention, and ultimately their intention was so upright that they gave their lives in preaching and martyrdom. Do not be afraid! [. . .] "Speak with your spiritual father, speak with your formators, pray, pray, pray, and you will see that the uprightness of your intention will grow and progress."

And this journey means meditating on the Gospel every day in order to transmit it by your life and preaching. It means experiencing the mercy of

God in the sacrament of reconciliation. Never omit this! Always go to confession! And thus shall you become generous and merciful ministers because you will feel God's mercy upon you. It means nourishing yourselves with faith and love for the Eucharist in order to nourish the Christian people. It means being men of prayer so as to become the voice of Christ praising the Father and interceding continually for the fellowship (cf. Heb. 7:25). The prayer of intercession, that made by those great men—Moses, Abraham—who contended with God for the people, that courageous prayer before God.

If you—but I say this from the heart, without wishing to give offence—if you, if someone among you is not ready to follow this path, with these attitudes and these experiences, it is better that you have the courage to seek another path. There are many ways in the Church of bearing Christian witness, and there are many paths that lead to holiness. In following as a minister of Jesus Christ, there is no place for mediocrity, that mediocrity that always leads to using the People of God to one's own advantage. Woe to the bad shepherds who feed themselves and not the flock!—the Prophets so forcefully exclaimed (cf. Ezek. 34:1–6)! And Augustine takes up this prophetic phrase in his *De Pastoribus*, which I recommend you read and meditate upon.

But woe to the bad shepherds, because the seminary, to tell the truth, is not a refuge for the many limitations we might have, a refuge for psychological defects or a refuge because I don't have the courage to go on with life and I am looking for a place to protect me. No, it is not this. If your seminary were this, it would become an apothecary of the Church! No, the seminary is intended precisely to move you forward, proceeding along this path. And when we hear the prophets say *woe!*, may this *woe!* make you reflect seriously on your future. Pius XI once said that it was better to lose a vocation than risk accepting an unsure candidate. He was a mountain climber; he knew about these things. [. . .]

33

The Priestly Joy

Homily at the Holy Chrism Mass, April 17, 2014

[. . .] [I]n the eternal "today" of Holy Thursday, when Christ showed his love for us to the end (cf. John 13:1), we recall the happy day of the institution of the priesthood, as well as the day of our own priestly ordination. The Lord anointed us in Christ with the oil of gladness, and this anointing invites us to accept and appreciate this great gift: the gladness, the joy of being a priest. Priestly joy is a priceless treasure, not only for the priest himself but for the entire faithful People of God, that faithful people from which he is called to be anointed and which he, in turn, is sent to anoint.

We are anointed with the oil of gladness so as to anoint others with the oil of gladness. Priestly joy has its source in the Father's love, and the Lord wishes the joy of this love to be "ours" and to be "complete" (John 15:11). I like to reflect on joy by contemplating Our Lady, for Mary, the "Mother of the living Gospel, is a wellspring of joy for God's little ones" (*Evangelii Gaudium*, 288). I do not think it is an exaggeration to say that a priest is very little indeed: the incomparable grandeur of the gift granted us for the ministry sets us among the least of men. The priest is the poorest of men unless Jesus enriches him by his poverty, the most useless of servants unless Jesus calls him his friend, the most ignorant of men unless Jesus patiently teaches him as he did Peter, the frailest of Christians unless the Good Shepherd strengthens him in the midst of the flock. No one is more "little" than a priest left to his own devices; and so our prayer of protection against every snare of the Evil One is the prayer of our Mother: I am a priest because he has regarded my littleness (cf. Luke 1:48). And in that littleness we find our joy. [. . .]

For me, there are three significant features of our priestly joy. It is a joy that *anoints us*, it is a joy that is *imperishable*, and it is a *missionary* joy that spreads and attracts, starting backward—with those farthest away from us.

A joy that anoints us. This joy has penetrated deep within our hearts; it has shaped them and strengthened them sacramentally. The signs of the ordination liturgy speak to us of the Church's maternal desire to pass on and share with others all that the Lord has given us: the laying on of hands, the anointing with sacred chrism, the clothing with sacred vestments, the first consecration which immediately follows. . . . Grace fills us to the brim and overflows, fully, abundantly and entirely in each priest. We are anointed down to our very bones . . . and our joy, which wells up from deep within, is the echo of this anointing.

An imperishable joy. The fullness of the gift, which no one can take away or increase, is an unfailing source of joy: an imperishable joy that the Lord has promised no one can take from us (cf. John 16:22). It can lie dormant or be clogged by sin or by life's troubles; yet deep down it remains intact, like the embers of a burnt log beneath the ashes, and it can always be renewed. Paul's exhortation to Timothy remains ever timely: I remind you to fan into flame the gift of God that is within you through the laying on of my hands (cf. 2 Tim. 1:6).

A missionary joy. I would like especially to share with you and to stress this third feature: priestly joy is deeply bound up with God's holy and faithful people, for it is an eminently missionary joy. Our anointing is meant for anointing God's holy and faithful people: for baptizing and confirming them, healing and sanctifying them, blessing, comforting, and evangelizing them.

And because this joy is one that springs up only when the shepherd is in the midst of his flock (for even in the silence of his prayer, the shepherd who worships the Father is with his sheep), it is a "guarded joy," watched over by the flock itself. Even in those gloomy moments when everything looks dark and a feeling of isolation takes hold of us, in those moments of listlessness and boredom that at times overcome us in our priestly life (and which I, too, have experienced), even in those moments God's people are able to "guard" that joy; they are able to protect you, to embrace you and to help you open your heart to find renewed joy.

All who are called should know that genuine and complete joy does exist in this world. It is the joy of being taken from the people we love and then being sent back to them as dispensers of the gifts and counsels of Jesus.

A "guarded joy": one guarded by the flock but also guarded by three sisters who surround it, tend it, and defend it: sister poverty, sister fidelity, and sister obedience.

The joy of priests is a joy that is sister to poverty. The priest is poor in terms of purely human joy. He has given up so much! And because he is poor, he, who gives so much to others, has to seek his joy from the Lord and from God's faithful people. He doesn't need to try to create it for himself. We know that our people are very generous in thanking priests for their slightest blessing and especially for the sacraments. Many people, in speaking of the crisis of priestly identity, fail to realize that identity presupposes belonging. There is no identity—and consequently joy of life—without an active and unwavering sense of belonging to God's faithful people (cf. *Evangelii Gaudium*, 268).

The priest who tries to find his priestly identity by soul-searching and introspection may well encounter nothing more than "exit" signs, signs that say, exit from yourself, exit to seek God in adoration, go out and give your people what was entrusted to you, for your people will make you feel and taste who you are, what your name is, what your identity is, and they will make you rejoice in that hundredfold which the Lord has promised to those who serve him. Unless you "exit" from yourself, the oil grows rancid and the anointing cannot be fruitful. Going out from ourselves presupposes self-denial; it means poverty.

Priestly joy is a joy that is sister to fidelity. Not primarily in the sense that we are all "immaculate" (would that by God's grace we were!), for we are sinners, but in the sense of an ever-renewed fidelity to the one Bride, to the Church. Here fruitfulness is key. The spiritual children which the Lord gives each priest, the children he has baptized, the families he has blessed and helped on their way, the sick he has comforted, the young people he catechizes and helps to grow, the poor he assists . . . all these are the "Bride" whom he rejoices to treat as his supreme and only love and to whom he is constantly faithful. It is the living Church, with a first name and a last name, that the priest shepherds in his parish or in the mission entrusted to him. That mission brings him joy whenever he is faithful to it, whenever he does all that he has to do and lets go of everything that he has to let go of, as long as he stands firm amid the flock the Lord has entrusted to him: "Feed my sheep" (cf. John 21:16, 17).

Priestly joy is a joy that is sister to obedience. I speak of an obedience to the Church in the hierarchy that gives us, as it were, not simply the external framework for our obedience: the parish to which I am sent, my ministerial assignments, my particular work . . . but also union with God the Father, the source of all fatherhood. It is likewise an obedience to the Church in service: in availability and readiness to serve everyone, always and as best I can, following the example of "Our Lady of Promptness" (cf. Luke 1:39, *meta spoudés*), who hastens to serve Elizabeth her kinswoman and is concerned for the kitchen of Cana when the wine runs out. The availability of her priests makes the Church a house with open doors, a refuge for sinners, a home for people living on the streets, a place of loving care for the sick, a camp for the young, a classroom for catechizing children about to make their First Communion. . . . Wherever God's people have desires or needs, there is the priest, who knows how to listen (*ob-audire*) and feels a loving mandate from Christ, who sends him to relieve that need with mercy or to encourage those good desires with resourceful charity.

All who are called should know that genuine and complete joy does exist in this world. It is the joy of being taken from the people we love and then being sent back to them as dispensers of the gifts and counsels of Jesus, the one Good Shepherd who, with deep compassion for all the little ones and the outcasts of this earth, wearied and oppressed like sheep without a shepherd, wants to associate many others to his ministry so as himself to remain with us and to work, in the person of his priests, for the good of his people.

[. . .] I ask the Lord Jesus to enable many young people to discover that burning zeal that joy kindles in our hearts as soon as we have the stroke of boldness needed to respond willingly to his call.

[. . .] I ask the Lord Jesus to preserve the joy sparkling in the eyes of the recently ordained who go forth to devour the world, to spend themselves fully in the midst of God's faithful people, rejoicing as they prepare their first homily, their first Mass, their first baptism, their first confession. . . . It is the joy of being able to share with wonder, and for the first time as God's anointed, the treasure of the Gospel and to feel the faithful people anointing you again and in yet another way: by their requests, by bowing their heads for your blessing, by taking your hands, by bringing you their children, by pleading for their sick. . . . Preserve, Lord, in your young priests the joy of going forth, of doing everything as if for the first time, the joy of spending their lives fully for you.

[. . .] I ask the Lord Jesus to confirm the priestly joy of those who have already ministered for some years. The joy which, without leaving their eyes, is also found on the shoulders of those who bear the burden of the ministry, those priests who, having experienced the labors of the apostolate, gather their strength and re-arm themselves—"get a second wind," as the athletes say. Lord, preserve the depth, wisdom, and maturity of the joy felt by these older priests. May they be able to pray with Nehemiah, "The joy of the Lord is my strength" (cf. Neh. 8:10).

Finally, [. . .] I ask the Lord Jesus to make better known the joy of elderly priests, whether healthy or infirm. It is the joy of the cross, which springs from the knowledge that we possess an imperishable treasure in perishable earthen vessels. May these priests find happiness wherever they are; may they experience already, in the passage of the years, a taste of eternity (Guardini). May they know, Lord, the joy of handing on the torch, the joy of seeing new generations of their spiritual children, and of hailing the promises from afar, smiling and at peace, in that hope that does not disappoint.

34

Bishops, Witnesses of the Risen One

Address at a meeting of the Congregation for Bishops,
February 27, 2014

In every age and in every place we shall receive this petition from the lips of the Church: give us a bishop! The holy People of God continues to speak: we need one who will watch over us from above; we need one who will see us with the fullness of God's heart. We do not need a *manager*, a chief executive officer of a company, [or] one who remains at the level of our pettiness and little pretensions. We need someone who knows how to raise himself to the heights of God's gaze over us in order to lead us to him. Our future lies in God's gaze. We need someone who, owing to his greater familiarity with the wide expanses of God's field than with the confines of his own narrow garden, is able to assure us that what our hearts aspire to is not a vain promise.

People toil the plains of everyday life and need to be guided by those who are able to see things from above. Therefore, we must never lose sight of the needs of the particular churches for which we provide. There is no *standard* pastor for all the churches. Christ knows the unique qualities of the pastor that each church requires, so that he can respond to its needs and help it realize its full potential. Our challenge is to enter into Christ's perspective, keeping in mind the uniqueness of the particular churches.

In order to choose such ministers, we all need to raise ourselves, climb to "higher levels." We cannot help but go up; we cannot be content with lower standards. We must rise over and above our own varied preferences, likes, affiliations, or tendencies in order to enter the expanse of God's horizon and to find those who bear his gaze from above. Not men conditioned by petty fears from below, but rather pastors endowed with *parrhesia*, who are able to ensure that a sacrament of unity exists (*Lumen Gentium*, no. 1) in the world and that humanity is therefore not destined for dispersion and confusion. [. . .]

Let us therefore examine the moment in which the Apostolic Church had to reassemble the College of the Twelve after Judas's betrayal. Without the Twelve, the fullness of the Holy Spirit could not descend. The successor is sought among those who followed Jesus' journey from the beginning and now could become, "together with the Twelve," a "witness to his resurrection" (cf. Acts 1:21–22). The witnesses of the Risen One had to be selected from among those who had followed Jesus.

> There is no standard pastor for all the churches. Christ knows the unique qualities of the pastor that each church requires, so that he can respond to its needs and help it realize its full potential.

From this derives the essential criterion for sketching the profile of the bishops we want to have. Who is a witness to the Risen One? It is the one who has followed Jesus from the beginning and who is established with the apostles as a witness to his resurrection. This is also a unifying criterion for us: the bishop is the one able to make all that happened to Jesus relevant today, and above all he knows, *together* with the Church, how to be a witness to his resurrection.

The bishop is first and foremost a martyr for the Risen One. He does not stand alone as a witness but stands together with the Church. His life and ministry must make the resurrection credible. In becoming one with Christ in the cross of the true gift of himself, he makes the life that never dies flow forth for his Church. The courage to die and the generosity to offer his life and to expend himself for the flock are inscribed in the "DNA" of the bishop. Renunciation and sacrifice are connatural with the mission of the bishop. And I wish to emphasize this: renunciation and sacrifice are connatural with the mission of the bishop. The episcopate does not exist for itself but for the

Church, for the flock, for others, especially for those whom the world would throw away.

Therefore, to identify a bishop, a list of human, intellectual, cultural, and even pastoral qualities is not useful. The profile of a bishop is not the algebraic sum of his virtues. Certainly he must be outstanding (*CIC*, can. 378 § 1); his human integrity ensures his capacity for healthy, balanced relationships so as not to project his own shortcomings onto others and become an element of instability. His Christian soundness is essential for promoting fellowship and communion. His upright behavior attests to the high standard of the disciples of the Lord. His cultural preparation allows him to dialogue with people and their cultures. His orthodoxy and fidelity to the truth whole and integral, which the Church safeguards, makes of him a pillar and point of reference. His interior and exterior discipline allow for self-mastery and open up opportunities for welcoming and leading others. His ability to govern with paternal firmness ensures the safety of the authority that leads to growth. His transparency and detachment in the administrations of the goods of the community invest him with authority and meet with the esteem of all.

All of these indispensable gifts must nonetheless be secondary to the central witness to the Risen One, subordinate to this primary commitment. It is the Spirit of the Risen One who fashions his witnesses, who integrates and elevates their qualities and value in fashioning a bishop.

35

Making Church While Walking

Address to the participants in the plenary assembly of the Pontifical Council for Social Communications, September 21, 2013

I would like to share some thoughts with you.

First: *the importance that the Church attaches to the area of communication.* This year is the fiftieth anniversary of the Conciliar Decree *Inter Mirifica.* This anniversary is more than a commemoration; the Decree expresses the Church's solicitude for communication in all its forms, which are important tools in the work of evangelization. There is a difference between these forms, which are functional means of communication, and communication itself, which is something else entirely. In the past few decades, the various means of communication have evolved significantly, but the Church's concern remains the same, though it assumes new ways of expression.

The world of communications, more and more, has become an "environment" for many, one in which people communicate with one another, expanding their possibilities for knowledge and relationship (cf. Benedict XVI, Message for the 2013 World Communications Day). I wish to underline these positive aspects, notwithstanding the limits and the harmful factors that also exist and that we are all aware of.

In this context—and this is my second point—we must ask ourselves, *what role should the Church have* in terms of the practical means of communication at her disposal? In every situation, beyond technological considerations, I believe that the goal is to understand how *to enter into dialogue with*

124

the men and women of today, to know how to engage this dialogue in order to appreciate their desires, their doubts, and their hopes. They are men and women who sometimes feel let down by a Christianity that to them appears sterile and in difficulty as it tries to communicate the depth of meaning that comes with the gift of faith.

We do in fact witness today, in the age of globalization, a growing sense of disorientation and isolation; we see, increasingly, a loss of meaning to life, an inability to connect with a "home," and a struggle to build meaningful relationships. It is therefore important to know how to dialogue and, with discernment, to use modern technologies and social networks in such a way as to reveal a presence that listens, converses, and encourages.

Allow yourselves, without fear, to be this presence, expressing your Christian identity as you become citizens of this environment. A Church that follows this path learns how to walk with everyone. There is an ancient rule for pilgrims, which St. Ignatius adopts, and which is why I know it! In one of his rules he says that the person accompanying the pilgrim must walk at his

> *Can we walk alongside the pilgrim of today's world as Jesus walked with those companions to Emmaus, warming their hearts on the way and bringing them to an encounter with the Lord?*

or her pace, not going on ahead or falling behind. In other words, I envision a Church that knows how to walk with men and women along the path. The pilgrim's rule will help inspire us.

The third thought: this is a challenge we must all face together in this environment of communications, where the issues are not principally technological. We must ask ourselves, are we up to the task of bringing Christ into this area, or better still, of *bringing others to meet Christ*? Can we walk alongside the pilgrim of today's world as Jesus walked with those companions to Emmaus, warming their hearts on the way and bringing them to an encounter with the Lord? Are we able to communicate the face of a Church that is "home" to all? We sometimes speak of a Church that has its doors closed, but here we are contemplating much more than a Church with open doors, much more! We must, together, build this "home," build this Church, make this "home." A Church with closed doors or open doors—the task is to move forward and help build the Church.

The challenge is to rediscover, through the means of social communication as well as by personal contact, the beauty that is at the heart of our existence and journey, the beauty of faith and of encounter with Christ. Even in this world of communications, the Church must warm the hearts of men and women. Do our presence and plans measure up to this requirement, or do we remain technicians? We hold a precious treasure that is to be passed on, a treasure that brings light and hope. They are greatly needed.

All this, however, means that priests, religious, and laity must have a thorough and adequate formation. The great digital continent not only involves technology but [also] is made up of real men and women who bring with them their hopes, their suffering, their concerns, and their pursuit of what is true, beautiful, and good. We need to bring Christ to others, through these joys and hopes, like Mary, who brought Christ to the hearts of men and women. We need to pass through the clouds of indifference without losing our way; we need to descend into the darkest night without being overcome and disorientated; we need to listen to the dreams without being seduced; we need to share their disappointments without becoming despondent; to sympathize with those whose lives are falling apart without losing our own strength and identity (cf. Pope Francis, Address to the Bishops of Brazil, 27 July 2013, n. 4). This is the path. This is the challenge.

It is important, dear friends, to bring the solicitude and the presence of the Church into the world of communications so as to dialogue with the men and women of today and bring them to meet Christ. But it is an encounter that is personal; it is not to be manipulated. Today there exists in the Church a great temptation that is a spiritual form of "abuse": to manipulate the mind—a sort of theological brainwashing that ultimately brings one to a superficial meeting with Christ but not to an encounter with the Person of Christ Alive! Within this encounter, there is the person, and there is Christ. There is no room for the spiritual engineer who wishes to manipulate.

This is the challenge: to bring the person to Christ. This must be done, however, in complete awareness that we ourselves are means of communication and that the real problem does not concern the acquisition of the latest technologies, even if these make a valid presence possible. It is necessary to be absolutely clear that the God in whom we believe, who loves all men and women intensely, wants to reveal himself through the means at our disposal, however poor they are, because it is he who is at work, he who transforms and saves us.

36

The Church Is Alive If It Astounds

Regina Coeli *address on the Solemnity of Pentecost, June 8, 2014*

The Feast of Pentecost commemorates the outpouring of the Holy Spirit on the apostles gathered in the Upper Room. Like Easter, this event took place on a preexisting Jewish feast and ended with a surprise. The Acts of the Apostles describes the signs and fruits of that extraordinary outpouring: the strong wind and tongues of fire; fear disappeared, leaving courage in its place; tongues melted and everyone understood the message. Wherever the Spirit of God reaches, everything is reborn and transfigured. Pentecost is the event that signals the birth of the Church and her public manifestation, and two features strike us: the Church *astounds* and *confuses*.

A fundamental element of Pentecost is *astonishment*. Our God is a God of astonishment; this we know. No one expected anything more from the disciples: after Jesus' death they were a small, insignificant group of defeated orphans of their Master. There occurred instead an unexpected event that astounded: the people were astonished because each of them heard the disciples speaking in their own tongues, telling of the great works of God (cf. Acts 2:6–7, 11). The Church born at Pentecost is an astounding community because, with the force of her arrival from God, a new message is proclaimed—the resurrection of Christ—with a new language, the universal one of love. A new proclamation: Christ lives, he is risen. A new language: the language of love. The disciples are adorned with power from above and speak with courage. Only minutes before, they all were cowardly, but now they speak with courage and candor, with the freedom of the Holy Spirit.

Thus the Church is called into being forever, capable of astounding while proclaiming to all that Jesus Christ has conquered death, that God's arms are always open, that his patience is always there awaiting us in order to heal us, to forgive us. The risen Jesus bestowed his Spirit on the Church for this very mission.

Take note: if the Church is alive, she must always surprise.

Take note: if the Church is alive, she must always surprise. It is incumbent upon the living Church to astound. A Church that is unable to astound is a Church that is weak, sick, dying, and that needs admission to the intensive care unit as soon as possible!

Some in Jerusalem would have liked Jesus' disciples, frozen in fear, to remain locked inside so as not to create *confusion*. Even today, many would like this from the Christians. Instead, the risen Lord pushes them into the world: "As the Father has sent me, even so I send you" (John 20:21). The Church of Pentecost is a Church that won't submit to being powerless, too "distilled." No, she doesn't submit to this! She doesn't want to be a decoration. She is a Church that doesn't hesitate to go out, meet the people, proclaim the message that's been entrusted to her, even if that message disturbs or unsettles the conscience, even if that message perhaps brings problems and sometimes leads to martyrdom. She is born one and universal, with a distinct identity, but open, a Church that embraces the world but doesn't seize it. She sets it free but embraces it like the colonnade in this Square: two arms that open to receive but that don't close to detain. We Christians are free, and the Church wants us free!

We turn to the Virgin Mary, who in that Pentecost morning was in the Upper Room, the Mother with her children. In her, the force of the Holy Spirit truly accomplished "great things" (Luke 1:49). She herself said so. May she, the Mother of the Redeemer and Mother of the Church, obtain through her intercession a renewed outpouring of God's Spirit upon the Church and upon the world.

Essential Chronology of
POPE FRANCIS'S *Life*

1936
17 December Born Jorge Mario Bergoglio in Buenos Aires into a family originally from Marche (Italy) who had immigrated to Argentina. Mario, his father, was an accountant in the railway company; Regina Sivori, his mother, was a homemaker. Jorge was the first of five children; his siblings are Óscar, Marta, Alberto, and María Elena.

1957
After achieving his diploma in chemistry, chose to become a priest and started seminary in Villa Devoto.

1960
12 March Took his First Vows.

1963
After completing humanities studies in Santiago, Chile, returned to Argentina, earning his philosophy degree at San José College in San Miguel.

1970
Finished his theological studies and graduated from San José College.

1930	1950	1960	1970

1958
11 March Started his novitiate at the Society of Jesus.

1964–66
Taught literature and psychology, first in Santa Fé and then in Buenos Aires.

1969
13 December Ordained a priest.

1973
22 April Made his Final Vows.

31 July After having been consultor, became Provincial Superior of Argentina's Jesuits.

1992

20 May After Bergoglio served for several years as spiritual director and confessor, John Paul II appointed him Auxiliary Bishop of Buenos Aires. Worked closely with Cardinal Antonio Quarracino, from whom he received episcopal ordination (27 June). Chose as his motto *Miserando atque eligendo* ("Having mercy, He chose him") and inserted the Christogram IHS, symbol of the Society of Jesus, into his coat of arms.

1993

21 December Appointed Vicar General of the Archdiocese of Buenos Aires.

2013

11 February Benedict XVI announced he would relinquish the Petrine ministry at the end of the month.

13 March Elected the new Supreme Pontiff, choosing the name *Francis*—he is the first Latin American pope, the first Jesuit pope, and the first to take the name *Francis*.

7 April Took his seat as Bishop of Rome on the Cathedra Romana.

24 June Created a pontifical commission to investigate the Institute for Works of Religion (the Vatican Bank).

29 June First encyclical *Lumen Fidei* published, thus completing the document Benedict XVI bequeathed to him.

2014

22 February Held his first consistory and appointed 19 new cardinals.

27 April Canonization of Blesseds John XXIII and John Paul II

13 August Made Apostolic Journey to the Republic of Korea for Sixth Asian Youth Day.

5–14 October Called his first Synod of the Bishops to discuss "The Pastoral Challenges of the Family in the Context of Evangelization."

1980 | 1990–2000 | 2013 | 2014–2015

1980

Appointed Rector of San José College, where he worked until 1986, when he stepped down to study theology in Germany and research Romano Guardini for his doctoral dissertation. His studies in Germany were interrupted by a summons from his Superiors in Argentina to take up other ministries. Ministered as a priest in a parish in Córdoba.

1997

3 June Promoted to Coadjutor Archbishop of Buenos Aires. Upon Cardinal Quarracino's death a year later, succeeded him in leading the Archdiocese (28 February) and became the Primate of Argentina.

2001

21 February Created a cardinal by John Paul II.

2005

Took part in the conclave electing Benedict XVI.

2013

8 July Made a historic visit to the island of Lampedusa.

22–29 July Took part in World Youth Day in Rio de Janeiro, Brazil.

22 September Made pastoral visit to Cagliari.

28 September Established the Council of Cardinals, tasked with advising Francis on ruling the Universal Church and starting reorganization of the apostolic constitution *Pastor bonus*, regarding the role of the Roman Curia.

4 October Made pastoral visit to Assisi.

24 November Apostolic exhortation *Evangelii Gaudium* published.

2015

15–19 January Made pastoral visit to the Philippines, where his final Mass was attended by 6 million people.

List of Sources

Part One: The Gospel of the Walk

1 A Journey Unfolding in Time: *Lumen Fidei*, June 29, 2013, nos. 18–22 (www.vatican.va).

2 The Eternal Newness of the Gospel: *Evangelii Gaudium*, November 24, 2013, n. 11 (www.vatican.va).

3 Three Movements of the Christian Life: Homily for the Mass with the cardinals, March 14, 2013 (www.vatican.va).

4 Walking with Jesus: Homily at the Public Consistory for the Creation of New Cardinals, February 22, 2014 (www.vatican.va).

5 The Joy of Encounter: *Evangelii Gaudium*, November 24, 2013, nos. 1–3 (www.vatican.va).

Part Two: The Walk of Faith

6 The Sacraments: Life and Sustenance for the Way: *Lumen Fidei*, June 29, 2013, nos. 40–45 (www.vatican.va).

7 Baptism: The Beginning: General Audience, January 8, 2014 (www.vatican.va).

8 Grace from Generation to Generation: General Audience, January 15, 2014 (www.vatican.va).

9 Confirmation: Crucial to Our Continuing: General Audience, January 29, 2014 (www.vatican.va).

10 The Eucharist: Sacrament of Love: General Audience, February 5, 2014 (www.vatican.va).

11 Living the Eucharist: General Audience, February 12, 2014
(www.vatican.va).

12 Reconciliation: The Power of Forgiveness: General Audience, February 19, 2014 (www.vatican.va).

13 Anointing the Sick: God's Compassion as We Persevere: General Audience, February 26, 2014 (www.vatican.va).

14 Religious Vocations: Walking in Service: General Audience, March 26, 2014 (www.vatican.va).

15 Christian Marriage: Walking in Covenant: General Audience, April 2, 2014 (www.vatican.va).

Part Three: The Gifts of the Walk

16 Holy Spirit: Our Companion on the Way: Homily, June 8, 2014
(www.vatican.va).

17 Walking with Wisdom: General Audience, April 9, 2014
(www.vatican.va).

18 Walking with Understanding: General Audience, April 30, 2014
(www.vatican.va).

19 Walking with Good Counsel: General Audience, May 7, 2014
(www.vatican.va).

20 Walking with Fortitude: General Audience, May 14, 2014
(www.vatican.va).

21 Walking with Knowledge: General Audience, May 21, 2014
(www.vatican.va).

22 Walking with True Piety: General Audience, June 4, 2014
(www.vatican.va).

23 Walking in the Fear of the Lord: General Audience, June 11, 2014
(www.vatican.va).

Part Four: The Witness of the Walk

24 Inviting Others to Walk with Us: *Lumen Fidei*, June 29, 2013,
nos. 37–39 (www.vatican.va).

Part Five: To Accompany on the Walk

Learn More About Pope Francis and His Message of Mercy

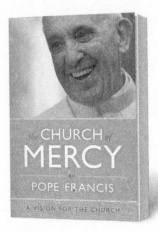

The Church of Mercy
A Vision for the Church

Collected from Pope Francis's speeches, homilies, and papers presented during the first year of his papacy, *The Church of Mercy* is the first Vatican-authorized book detailing his vision for the Catholic Church. This book's deep wisdom reminds us that the Church must move beyond its own walls and joyfully bring God's mercy wherever suffering, division, or injustice exists.

Hardcover | 4168-0 | $22.95
Paperback | 4170-3 | $16.95
Discussion Guide 10-Pack | 4204-5 | $9.95

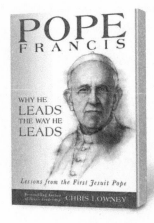

Pope Francis: Why He Leads the Way He Leads
Lessons from the First Jesuit Pope

Best-selling author and former Jesuit seminarian Chris Lowney offers an in-depth look at how Pope Francis's Jesuit training has directly impacted his various leadership roles and what it suggests about how he might lead in the future. Readers will gain essential lessons to help them with their own leadership challenges.

Hardcover | 4008-9 | $22.95
Paperback | 4091-1 | $16.95

TO ORDER: Call 800.621.1008, visit www.loyolapress.com/store, or visit your local bookseller.